LAST CALL, STUPID

AN EXIT SRATEGY FROM TOXIC DRINKING CULTURE

First edition
Designed by Trey Derbes

CONTENTS

No matter who you are or where you are in life, consider these pages a wink, a hug, and a kiss on the cheek along your journey. If the world has knocked the wind out of you, I want this to be a breath of life into your lungs. Let this give you the strength, confidence, and courage to spit back into the face of adversity. Am I doing the best I can? Am I heading in the right direction? You are not alone in your feelings of self-doubt and uncertainty about where you belong in the cosmos.

I wish I could say I have all the answers for you. I don't. Nobody does. Be wary of those trying to sell you a cure or believe they have some ultimate higher truth. Be skeptical of any system with a standardized, cookie-cutter way of telling you who you are and how they will fix you. If you have ever been looked at with smug, cynical judgment and discarded as irredeemable, I want you to know that you matter. This is a clenched fist and an emphatic *FUCK YOU* to anyone, anything, and any substance that tries to take your heart and spirit from you.

The only thing we can do is try our best and correct course from our mistakes. Remember to keep a smile and song in your heart even when life is cruel and unfair. Don't take anything personally, and be authentically and unapologetically you. Embrace new experiences, laugh, help, be kind, brighten someone's day, and don't take anything too seriously. The number of days left in our lives is uncertain. Live passionately, and live NOW!

~ DEDICATIONS ~

To my family ~ Thank you for helping me in any way you could, even when I didn't deserve it. I know I wasn't the easiest kid to raise. I will always appreciate how you made sure I had something to eat and a couple of extra bucks in my pocket when things were tough for me. Your individual initials are tattooed over my heart for a reason. Every act of love and kindness you've shown me has not gone unappreciated.

Mike ~ You have been my surrogate, cooler older brother that I always looked up to. Your character and attitude toward life have always been a North Star for me. Thank you for your help, support, and friendship.

Trey ~ You have been my brother throughout the decades. We've seen each other in the best and worst times. Your friendship and presence in my life are significant beyond articulation. Thanks for sticking with me.

Mikaela ~ You have been an unending well of love, support, and advice that has kept me afloat over the years. Without your help and encouragement, this book may have never seen the light of day. My respect and adoration for you are immeasurable. Thank you for being you.

Shawna ~ Thank you for being a ray of sunshine and making me smile. Our conversations and time together have always made me glow a little brighter. Thanks for remembering more of my stories than I do.

Grace ~ No apology I could ever utter would be enough to tell you how sorry I am for my behavior. Your allowing me to remain your friend is a testament to your graciousness and generous heart. I'm forever in your debt.

Rachel ~ You unwittingly became the catalyst that changed my life completely. Without your role in my story, I might not have made it out of the hole I was in. I'm genuinely sorry for all the headaches, heartaches, and disappointments.

Courtney ~ Your wisdom, compassion, and empathy are stunning. I learned more from you than you'll ever know. You are a remarkable, beautiful human being.

To all the people I've shared stages, vans, and studios with, it was my pleasure to play with you... Sweating out my heart and soul through sticks, strings, and breath with my fellow brothers and sisters has been the highlight of my existence. Music is a facet of my biology, and I thank you for letting me be a part of your songs, and you a part of mine. It has been an honor.

The universe brings people together and separates even the strongest of bonds. No matter the reason for our disconnect, the memories of our time together have made my life beautiful. The laughter, the wild nights, the conversations, and the time shared are priceless. I will always have love and a special place in my heart for so many of you. If you come across these words, I am grateful for your existence and hope there is joy and peace in your life. Thank you for being a part of me.

Thanks to every single person who has crossed my path during my life. Whether you loved, hated, or gave me no thought at all, you have impacted the person I am today.

And lastly, to everyone I've ever met, in the entirety of my years, I'm sorry if I was an asshole.

1

Dazed and Bruised

"No tree can grow to heaven unless its roots reach down to hell."

~ Carl Jung

It was hot out already. Too goddamn hot for such an early hour. It was an ordinary Tuesday morning in September, and I was in Los Feliz, a trendy Hollywood-adjacent neighborhood. Around 7:30 a.m., I slowly began to wake up. Fighting to open my eyes, it felt like tiny lead Christmas ornaments were hanging from my eyelashes. I was drenched in sweat—or at least what I hoped was sweat. The heat was even more despicable because I was sitting in the passenger seat of my car with the windows rolled up. Black pants down around my ankles. I was wearing a white dress shirt halfway unbuttoned and translucent from said mystery fluid. I'm not sure why I dressed myself like a waiter that night, but I guess that was the ensemble that spoke to me. It took a couple of seconds for me to realize I was also wearing a blood-soaked kitchen rag wrapped around my right wrist. *What the hell did I get myself into last night? Has anyone tried to get a hold of me? I was a twenty-something in the late 90's, so let me check my sweet, raspberry-red mini Motorola pager.*

I had that type of dry mouth that only gin and cocaine can provide. Luckily, a nice half-full, 24oz can of PBR was in the center console cup holder, still wrapped in a brown paper bag. Someone, or myself, had left me a hot breakfast; How thoughtful! I took a big ole swig of that motherfucker. I swished it around in my mouth to help clear the film that had solidified on my tongue and teeth overnight.

Feeling slightly less like a piece of shit, it was time to figure out where the hell I was. Let me get my bearings; my car was facing southeast, the optimal placement to get the full brunt of the sun's good morning slap across my face. There was a lot of foot traffic for a Sunday morning. *Oh, wait, it's Tuesday…I think…ugh…wait, what the fuck?! Why are there kids? Lots of them!* The little bastards were everywhere, skipping past my car with their carefree smiles and not-yet-soiled spirit of joy. Their happiness was still intact because the cognitive realization of their insignificance hadn't yet soured all their hopes and dreams. It was as if they were mocking me with their ability to make choices without suffering any real consequences.

My drunk self, or whoever was driving, had left me for dead in front of some sort of school. As the kids strolled by my car, I wondered if the tint on my window hid the vacant, confused stare just a few feet away from their innocent eyeballs. For a second, I had a vision that I had traveled back in time and saw myself walking onto campus. I wanted so badly to roll down my window and say, "Pssst, hey, kid…get ova here" and show my younger self how cool I had become and how good I smelled.

But It was time to get the fuck out of there. I pulled my damp pants up my sweaty legs, buttoned up my shirt, and scooched over the center console into the driver's seat. I lit a cigarette and immediately regretted it. That head rush, smell, and taste hit me like a frying pan upside the head. The first smoke when you wake up morbidly hungover is a vicious punch to the senses, but your addictions don't care about how you feel. They need to be indulged with or without your permission. With a freshly sparked butt dangling from my mouth, I grabbed my wayfarers from the dash, slapped them on my face, and was ready to go. The keys were still in the ignition in the "ON" position, which wasn't a good sign. I mumbled my prayers of "please turn on, please turn on" to the car gods, but they answered with a "fuuuuuuck you…we're not going anywhere! Your drunk ass left me on all night."

Well, hell… the battery is dead. Now why the fuck is my wrist bandaged up?

Trying to assemble the pieces through a foggy vision, I remembered being at a bar and climbing on top of a table to dance—only to have said table topple over, with me and all the drinks on it. Being a gentleman and a scholar, I tried to clean up my mess, only to be stabbed by a shard of glass. Then the establishment's manager pulled me into the kitchen, wrapped a rag around my wrist, stuffed a few packets of Neosporin in my pocket, and sent me on my way. I still can't stomach the smell of gin because of that night. As for how I wound up in the passenger seat of my car with my pants down, that remains an X-file.

Luckily, I knew where I was—and there was a liquor store and a service station nearby. Let us go on an adventure! I had to get something more refreshing to drink to kill this hangover. I didn't have any blow left in my bullet ("blow" being cocaine, and "bullet" being a cocaine dispenser), so Red Bull vodka it is—a little something to steady my hands and numb my head. After my stop at the liquor store, I needed to borrow some jumper cables from the service station. When I was walking up the driveway of the garage, I was getting "What the fuck is this guy's deal" kind of looks. I didn't wonder why the mechanic asked to hold my ID and a credit card as collateral. I certainly looked, felt, and had the aroma of a respectable, upstanding pillar of society. But you can never be too careful these days, especially in Hollywood.

With an ever so slight, cool stagger, I saunter down Franklin Avenue at 8:00 on a Tuesday morning with a drink in one hand and some jumper cables in the other. This "pick up the scraps of my life" scavenger hunt is going great so far. While walking, I occasionally tried to sneak in a sip of my beverage, but my motor skills weren't quite back to 100% yet, so I hit the can to my face like a dummy, splashing my impromptu cocktail down my chin.

Finally, I made it back to my car. I popped a fresh piece of gum into my ever-so-cottony cottonmouth, hoping it would gussy up my breath because at this point, it could peel paint off a wall. I opened the hood of my car and started to solicit the good favor of anyone willing to help. Fortunately, for this area, I don't look *too* shabby. Haggard? Yes. Hungover? Abso-fucking-lutely. But dangerous? Eh, not really. Just a run-of-the-mill degenerate and this town is full of them. Besides, how menacing can some Cheesecake Factory waiter, zombie-looking motherfucker be? I was holding jumper cables in front of a Toyota Celica with a sad look on my pathetic face. It didn't take too long for someone to come to my aid; say what you want about LA, there are still a few good ones out there. I got my jump and I'm ready to go! To where? Who the fuck cares! I just know I'm on my way.

To most, this might seem like a pretty glaring sign: "Hey, maybe we should pump the brakes on the ol' sauce, huh, kid?" Not me, motherfucker. I live for this shit! It was par for the course. Just a routine night turning into morning, morning turning into day, day turning into god-knows-what. Not a care in the world. The only thing that mattered was more, more, *more*! As a matter of fact, this was just a drop in the bucket of fucked-up starts to days. Consequences aren't considered when you're not frightened of the worst possible outcome.

I took pride in my catalog of depravity—the more gruesome, deviant, and sexually perverse the tale, the better. Waking up in jail makes for an interesting story. So does having a screwdriver jabbed between my ribs trying to buy crack in a donut shop parking lot. Would you rather hear about the time I got that big promotion, *or* do you want to hear about the time I was in a dark alley scoring meth from a prostitute who had both boobs and a wiener? Fun fact: Nothing accentuates a semi-flaccid dong better than a dayglow green mini-skirt.

Looking back at all the nonsense I've been through, I still can smile and laugh at it. I found a lot of good times at the bottom of a bottle and inhaled a lot of "fun" through a rolled-up bill. I've met many awesome, interesting people and had many adventures. I found myself in countless situations, both amazing and horrifying. These experiences changed my DNA. My perspectives. The fiber of my being. They are the reason why I'm writing whatever this is.

Of course, there is the other side of that coin, too. All the stupid shit I've done. The "Oh fuck, what did I do last night?" feeling in the morning. The painful memories that make me cringe, and still occasionally haunt my thoughts. I'm lucky not to remember all the details of what I've said and done, but some people know too well of all the reprehensible bullshit I'm guilty of, and what I've put them through. Friendships strained. Hearts broken. Embarrassment and shame. The indescribable, suffocating feeling of dread and impending doom. Ya know… All that fun shit!

I wouldn't consider myself a drug addict, but I definitely did a lot of drugs. And sure, I had several indicators that define the clinical definition of an alcoholic, but I don't think I reasonably fit that description either. The one thing that I have absolutely no doubt of is that I went fucking *hard*. I was at the party for twenty years. And it was pretty rad, but it was time to go. *How do I leave? Am I sure I want to leave? Where the fuck am I going to go now, and who's coming with me?*

I didn't feel obligated to stop drinking; it just felt like something I needed to do. There was no intervention or even a concerned chat from a loved one. Just an ever-increasing tiredness in my mind and spirit that longed for something else. I was finally starting to shed the skin of my young adulthood. My life was like Groundhog Day–a playlist on repeat. I was bored, exhausted, and sick of doing the same shit over and over again. I needed and wanted something to change for me, and I knew exactly what that "thing" was, but I was terrified to admit it. They say the catalyst for making a significant difference in your life is a breaking point. An "I'VE FUCKING HAD IT" moment. Well, friends, I had fucking had it!

Maybe you're too proud or embarrassed to admit that you have a problem. Maybe you are scared of giving up your "identity." Maybe you think partying hard is the last vestige of your youth–that you desperately cling to with visibly aged hands because you can't come to terms with letting it go yet. But maybe, you're also on the same sinking ship I was on and are too physically and mentally drained to keep it afloat. Even if it's difficult to tell your friends and family that you'd like their help, support, and understanding, the most important thing is that

You are ready.

You are sick of the bullshit.

You want to change.

Well my friends, I will tell you how I did it. I'm a very DIY, punk rock type of guy, which made finding resources and philosophies that resonated with me more complicated than you'd think. I want to share some of the things I've learned along the way, perspectives I've gained, and different paradigms to look through. I know I have some version of SUD (substance abuse disorder) but I didn't feel like I fit into any specific group, addiction-wise. I want to share my story in hopes it can help anyone who may need help. Perhaps this will put a mirror up to some of your behavior patterns that you didn't know you needed to confront. Take everything I say with a grain of salt. I'm not an addiction counselor, therapist, or cult leader. I have no credentials other than experience and scar tissue. I'm not selling a program or even total sobriety, for that matter. This is simply my story of how I stopped drinking; unconventional wisdom from an unconventional asshole.

It's last call, stupid… You don't have to leave, but you probably should.

Upbringing

"The best way to keep a prisoner from escaping is to ensure he never knows he's in prison."

~ Fyodor Dostoevsky

How did the Joker become the Joker? What in his upbringing made Hitler such a dick? What trauma did the inventor of the DMV sustain in their life to want to inflict such insufferable misery upon humanity? I don't know, man—I just drank a lot and did stupid shit. I have no tragic tale to tell. No abuse or broken home. Just an Average, middle-class family upbringing in suburbia.

I grew up in a smallish town called La Crescenta in the foothills of Los Angeles, about fifteen miles from downtown LA. My immediate family consists of a four-person crew: Mom, Dad (still married), a sister who is six years my senior, and me. We always had food, shelter, and gifts under the Christmas tree.

Pops was an auto mechanic. He sacrificed nearly all of his time for us, breaking his back, turning a wrench six days a week. Sometimes, after a full shift, he'd grind out an additional couple of hours to fix our cars. He did this without a complaint. As long as he had the big piece of chicken on his plate come dinner time, he seemed content. My mother was a stay-at-home mom who would have odd jobs here and there. She kept a beautiful home and ensured laundry was done, the yards were pristine and a delicious meal was waiting for us every night. On holidays, she decorated the house to the nines. My sister, who had a few years of maturity and wisdom on me, made me feel cooler—like I had inside knowledge of things only "older kids" knew. She is wickedly smart and taught me how to drive a car. These three unique individuals are kind, smart, funny, and have beautiful, generous hearts.

Alcohol was always around the house. It was always around everybody's house. There wasn't a friend or family member who didn't have a bottle of something somewhere, or a twelve-pack in a fridge out in the garage. There was nothing out of the ordinary in my household, and that's the biggest problem of them all. *The normalization of habitually consuming poison to elude the unpleasantness of subsistence.* Nightcaps during the week and binge drinking on the weekends are just what you do. It's this narrative, this illusion that most people cannot break free from. A spell they don't even know they are under. My folks are not alcoholics. On the weekends, they would ramp it up a bit, but they didn't get hammered every night. They would have their champagne and beer, but it wasn't in excess.

The golden, fizzy beverages always looked like a treat or reward as a kid. They were something you had earned for a long day of sweating underneath a hot, greasy car, maintaining a house, and keeping two kids alive. I remember begging my mom for a sip of her "Cold Duck champagne" or my dad for a nip of his

Budweiser. They'd usually always oblige. Sometimes, I'd even get my own little one-ounce glass they'd pour it into. In their defense, my parents were teens of the '60s—young adults of the '70s. Back then, we had heavy, skull-crushing lawn darts to play with and poisonous lead in our paint. For Christ's sake, you could smoke inside a Burger King or on a flight! It was a different, wild time. I'm not throwing anyone under the bus, there just wasn't easy access to information like there is now. After having a child, they didn't have the luxury of taking out their phone and asking: "Hey, Google, how do I not fuck this kid up?" If you wanted to research anything, you had to get to a library and do some digging. You also have to consider they grew up in a time when parents were even less informed about such hooey as "supportive emotional development" or "pediatric behavioral health." What a bunch of sissy, new-age bullshit!

Even without the little sips here and there, the glamourization of alcohol was and still is always present. The grooming process to be a drinker starts early on, and my young, absorbent brain was taking note of every last detail. All this data waiting to be recalled consciously or, even more fun, becoming a subconscious Trojan horse timebomb to enjoy later in life. I was taught by example that drinking was something to look forward to—a good thing. Every TV show, movie, commercial, print ad, etc., contributes to the glorification of drinking. It's ingrained in our culture, tattooed on the butt cheek of the human experience. Luckily, we can dismantle and reassemble these learned patterns into more productive behaviors. As the saying goes, "Tradition is just peer pressure from dead people."

Junior high was the first significant change that I can remember. Kindergarten through sixth grade, I was in the same elementary school with mostly the same kids for seven years. In seventh grade, I was thrown onto a new campus with many new faces. I now had my very own locker I could decorate and six different teachers to annoy, and everybody was figuring out the mysterious, forbidden magic of their genitals. Oh, what a time… what a terrible, horrible time.

I started playing drums and writing songs when I was eight. I was performing in talent shows by the sixth grade, making me a seasoned prepubescent pro by the time I entered the new school. I was a huge metalhead, listening to classics like Twisted Sister, Anthrax, Iron Maiden, and Metallica. In elementary school, I was the only one on campus with a passion and skill for rock music. Finally meeting other musicians into the same genre as me was amazing, and it didn't take long for me to find new friends. I just looked for long hair, ripped jeans, and band T-shirts, and before I knew it, I was in my very first band, "TORMENT." What does an eleven-year-old boy with raging hormones know better than torment?

Some kids partied in junior high, but there weren't a lot of them. Every school had one or two "burnouts" with tie-dyed shirts and horrible attendance, but we were all reasonably behaved. Sure, we were flirting with smoking cigarettes and maybe some pot. Beers, if we were lucky, but nothing harder than wine. Junior high was the first glimpse of partying, but nothing serious.

I did manage to get myself arrested for the first time at that age. My friend and I were having a sleepover at my parent's house and decided to sneak out and take a walk. A cop had driven by us, and we got spooked and ran because we were young and stupid. The police set up a perimeter, thinking we were car thieves. When they finally caught us and realized we were just eleven and twelve, they woke our parents up in the middle of the night to pick us up at the station. No charges were filed, and they let us go, but it sure scared my folks. Little did I know, I'd return to that police station several more times in my twenties.

Welcome to high school, motherfucker! Now this is where the real bad seeds are planted. Seeds that later grow into terrible, unsustainable, haunted forests filled with trees that become an ever-growing, inescapable labyrinth of questionable decisions and debilitating habits. Nights turning into weeks, weeks into years, years into decades, decades into finding yourself in your forties, hungover at a job you despise, living a life you hate while thinking about the youth you've squandered. (Individual results may vary.)

Oddly enough, I didn't drink or do drugs at all during my high school years. I didn't even smoke cigarettes. On my way out of junior high, I stumbled upon something much better. I found my one true love. Punk Rock Music! I was introduced to the Dead Kennedys, Circle Jerks, Minor Threat, Black Flag, The Misfits. It was time to take the dog clippers to this bullshit hippie hair and shave it into a mohawk!

The attitude, look, and sound of punk rock seemed tailor-made for me. The intelligence in the lyrics ignited a passion for going to the library and finding books that weren't prescribed in the standard American high school curriculum. I was sincerely trying to understand complex philosophies and theories for the first time, something that no previous teacher or class inspired me to do. There was nothing like sinking into my Bad Religion cassette tape with my dictionary handy and having myself a night.

Within the punk scene is a sub-genre called "straight edge" or Hardcore Straight Edge. HCSE punks didn't drink, smoke, do drugs, or have sex. (I never understood the "no sex" part, so I just ignored that rule.) I was an angsty teen, and it resonated with me deeply. When you're living that role, rebelling against your parents and the norms of society is part of the script—part of your character. Not drinking or doing drugs was about the most punk rock, contrarian thing I could do.

I don't recall ever getting a hard time for not partaking in any substances. I went to the parties, mainly because my band was playing them; seeing how fucked up and stupid people got was a turnoff, especially the idiotic shit like beer bongs and keg stands. Have you ever seen anyone "fish out" after huffing a balloon full of noz? Let me explain that—it's doing a "whippet" at a professional level. For a time in the '90s, tanks of noz, or nitrous oxide, were all the rage at parties. You would fill a giant balloon full of laughing gas and inhale the entire thing in one breath. The effect would be an exceptionally dizzying head rush that lasted about a minute. A funny side effect is that it has the opposite reaction to helium on your voice—it makes you sound like a super fucked-up cartoon version of Barry White. It would also sometimes make the person "enjoying" it immediately faint, fall to the ground, and convulse mildly. Hence, "fishing out."

But when you're that young, you don't care about much. You have simple needs that are met by simple ends. You're certainly not considering how much irreversible bodily damage, externally or internally, you could be doing. You're not concerned with the why you are doing this. Our teenage years solidify and validate how we see drinking.

Remember how the perception of alcohol is embedded in our

young, malleable brains? As teenagers, we come to know it does precisely what we've been led to believe. Not only is it cool to do, it disarms all those teenage insecurities. Maybe it's taking the edge off these difficult new emotions, *or maybe* it's making you forget about a bad home or school life, but whatever it's doing, it seems to be working. And at that age, it has very little consequence.

When high school ended, so did the band. Some members moved away for college or work, the others just gave up. Not me, man. I'm committed! A lifer! School and I didn't get along, so college wasn't in my future. I have a deep desire and love for learning and discovery, but the standard structure of the school system isn't accommodating for someone like me. F*uck that learning stuff, man! I'm gonna be a rockstar!* That's what I said to myself as I muled pizza in my '77 Mach 1, T-topped Mustang, still living at my parent's house at the ripe age of nineteen. That was my first job; I had no bills except for gas and cigarettes. ("Wait, cigarettes?" Oh yeah, my straight edginess will come to an end real soon. I told you it would happen.)

In my teens, my self-destructive behavior was growing roots in the form of body modifications. Sadomasochism 101, if you will. On my eighteenth birthday, I went to Tattoo Mania on the Sunset Strip and got my first taste of a tattoo gun. Back then, it wasn't as common as it is now so a tattoo was a pretty extreme thing to do. I remember my bandmate who accompanied me to the parlor saying afterward, "We better become fucking rockstars now!" As if no one would hire me because I was a tattooed, bona fide outcast of society, bearing the mark of a hardened criminal. You might be thinking, *Man, what did he get? A swastika on his face? A big veiny cock on his neck?* Nope, I got a one-inch Japanese kanji of the word "tranquility" on my wrist.

When I did start drinking, I did not gingerly dip my toe in first to see how the water was. I tied an anvil around my ankle and dove straight into the deep end. I already had a self-destructive, devil-may-care attitude mixed in with a flair for the dramatic, so adding liquor was like throwing napalm and gunpowder into a fire. I started drinking as a conscious decision, like an "I'm gonna give this a shot" type experiment. Much like when Bradley Nowell (singer of Sublime) consciously decided to do heroin because he thought that's the price you pay to the devil for the larger-than-life rockstar legend status. Unfortunately, he wasn't wrong. But I was getting into new territory with myself; I wanted to live the life! At some subconscious level, I'm sure I was also trying to self-medicate from the life I was already living, but I knew this was part of the deal, and I was ready to say, "Fuck it all, deal me in!" Let's push this as far as it can go.

I chose a bottle of E&J brandy for my first drink. At the time I was going through a retro phase and wanted to seem classy like Dean Martin and Frank Sinatra. See how that brainwashing works? Like Dino said, "Ain't that a kick in the head?" Little did I know I was about to embark on a twenty-year-long journey that I barely survived.

3

The Roaring Twenties & Thirties

"Life should not be a journey to the grave with the intention of arriving safely in a pretty and well preserved body, but rather to skid in broadside in a cloud of smoke, thoroughly used up, totally worn out, and loudly proclaiming "Wow! What a Ride!"

~ Hunter S. Thompson

I couldn't tell you why I gave up my straight-edge lifestyle, but I can tell you that I went from zero to this guy's got a fucking problem real' quick. I spent all my twenties and thirties drinking heavily and frequently; playing shows, touring, and hanging out at clubs, bars, and parties was how I spent my time. I also got into some trouble and went to jail on a few occasions. I almost killed myself and nearly got killed by other people. I went from job to job, partner to partner. I was on an emotional rollercoaster that took me to the highest highs and the lowest lows. Alcohol fueled everything that I did.

All the romanticizing and glorifying of the live fast, die young paradigm proved to be the siren's song that would beguile me to crash my ship into the rocks; and there were a lot of goddamn rocks! Beyond the rockstar, tortured artist, and lovable-lush types my impressionable mind wanted to emulate, I was also starting to pull at the thread of existential contemplation. I quickly found that alcohol and drugs were a respite from the ever-increasing weight and darkness of my thoughts. That is, until it started making it much worse and taking me to the deepest pits of hopelessness and despair I've ever wallowed in. But let's begin at the honeymoon phase, shall we?

I started drinking when I was nineteen. The lightness I felt without the weight of self-consciousness was liberating. All my filters and insecurities vanished, and any regard for my personal safety was rendered null and void. The boost of dopamine felt like a warm, comforting ray of sunshine in a perpetually dark and cloudy existence. *AH HA! This is why people drink! I get it now!*

One of my first memories of alcohol changing my perception of reality was the obligatory, overly enthusiastic "I love you, man!" bro fests. It's almost a rite of passage in a young adult male life. The booze gave me permission to be open and vulnerable and express emotion in an unconstrained fashion. What a fantastic feeling! Slurring out exaggerated terms of endearment to your best friends, acquaintances, strangers in dark allies, or anybody within earshot of me, felt great. Stumbling, carefree, down the street while whistling a jaunty tune was how I wanted to live. What the hell was I doing before being all sober and miserable? *Fuck that, man! This is way better!*

Throughout my life, I've played countless shows in several different bands, and I still play to this day. In my teens and twenties, I started performing at all the Hollywood bars and clubs, including The Whiskey, Roxy, and Troubadour. I've played all over the U.S. and Europe. I went on my first national tour when I was twenty-one. That was my first experience being drunk for thirty days straight. Band practices were usually two to three times per week and an excuse to drink a few eighteen-packs with my buddies. On show days, the amount of beer would double, and of course, there'd be shots and cocktails and whatever drugs I could get my hands on. While on the road, drinking twenty beers daily would be a politely modest estimate. If you want to do the math on that, I'd drink at least 560 beers in a four-week run, not including all the other goodies.

I started going to bars and hitting the LA Goth club scene when I was twenty. Alcohol dissolved my timidness. I was no longer afraid to approach or interact with anyone. I had also never danced at a club or in public before. I wasn't afraid to act crazy and passionate on stage playing music (I had been doing that since I was ten), but beyond that, I was, and still am, a little quiet and reserved. A few shots and several beers later, that shyness was nowhere to be found. I'd see myself on top of podiums, stages, and sometimes on top of dining tables and bars. Once, I found myself in the middle of an orgy in an *after* after-hours industrial bondage club, wearing nothing but a pair of women's leather pants. Another time, I somehow came in first place in a dance contest; I entered drunk, winning a carton of Newport cigarettes and a trip to Florida. There was no telling where I'd wind up. My fuck-it meter was cranked to ten, and it was amazing! Drinking seemed to make everything better. There was never a dull moment after some elicit beverages. I was in love with my new self.

Reckless, careless, arrogant, self-centered, and belligerent would be some choice adjectives that described me during this time. I was a paragon of scumbaggery. I made it my mission to be as shocking, outrageous, and obscene as I could. I got a kick out of freaking people out. Whether it be by piercing various body parts with safety pins in public or having my friends spit their chewed-up food directly into my mouth, feeding me like a bird. I'd put cigarettes out on myself, and sometimes I'd take my shirt off at bars, lay down on a table, and have anyone willing, pour hot candle wax over me. There wasn't much I wouldn't do to shock and disturb people. I also started doing idiotic shit like petty theft and vandalism, going on beer runs (going into a store and then running out with beer you've not paid for), setting various things on fire, and just being an all-around nuisance. Nothing major or maliciously criminal. I was more of a mischievous, pesky fellow.

One of my first memories of stupid behavior related to alcohol was when I was twenty and went into a grocery store very drunk, past 2:00 a.m. (the cut-off time to buy alcohol in California). I knew I couldn't purchase any more liquor, so I grabbed a bottle of Jack Daniels and drank it in their bathroom. I had passed out on the floor for a couple of hours and was awakened by one of the employees banging on the door. I slurred a "Sorry, man" and stumbled back into the night.

Situations like this were just the start. Besides grocery store restroom floors, I'd soon find myself waking up in all sorts of fun and unexpected locations: in strange beds next to strangers, in the bushes of parks, in cars (sometimes under them or in the trunk), in different geographical states, on the ground in alleyways and parking lots, or jail... Sometimes, I'd still have pants on; sometimes, not. If I was lucky, I remembered how I wound up in whatever predicament I was in, but usually, I had no recollection of how I landed where I did.

I thought it was all funny instead of problematic, a character-building exercise. I was never at a loss for a story about some drunken adventure I went on. I didn't have any real responsibilities yet, so I did as I pleased. Hangovers didn't exist in my twenties; it was pedal-to-the-floor debauchery. I could walk out of a bar at 2:00 a.m. and still make it to my 4:30 a.m. shift at my coffee shop. I'd still be pretty drunk, but I'll be damned if I wasn't the fastest barista west of the Mississippi! I started to feel invincible because my young body rebounded so quickly from all the abuse I put it through. I was becoming party Superman!

I was twenty-two when cocaine finally found me at some party in the Hollywood hills. I knew it would find me sooner or later, and sure enough, it was love at first snort. Holy smokes, what a magnificent beast this was to ride! Not only did I feel like the most amazingly competent, enthusiastic person on the planet, but I was no longer on the wrong side of drunk. The slurs went away. I could walk in a straight line. I was alert and coherent. I could drive a car better. Most importantly of all, I could drink more! My alcohol problem wasn't a problem at all; it just needed cocaine!

My party life became a lot more interesting. As If the drunk conversations weren't unintelligible enough, now I got to have them until 7:00 a.m. while speaking at 300 words per minute and smoking an entire pack of cigarettes. I was able to go into the "private rooms" at parties. I found that I was pretty popular if I had a couple of grams on me or had the hook-up for "party supplies." I got to rub elbows with multiple varieties of drug dealers, from middle-aged gay dudes with pet-attack parrots to sketchy, stabby gang members. I suddenly saw myself at the cool kid's table, occasionally doing blow with B-list celebrities. I wasn't a rich or famous rockstar, but fuck me if I didn't try to act the part and live the life.

Much like the ritual of smoking, I truly loved the whole process behind procuring and doing cocaine. It usually went as follows: The itch came around the third or fourth drink. At that point, I would see who was down to pitch in on a bag and then start making phone calls. When I made the contact, and the deal was a go, it was the best feeling on the goddamn planet! There was no obstacle too big to keep me away from picking up drugs once that bee had entered my bonnet. Finding a place to chop the first couple of lines and rolling up a bill to snort them up with always felt so cool; I ain't gonna lie. But, when the itch came, and nobody could scratch it, I became an overly anxious, annoying prick. I'm sure some nights, my dealer had a hundred missed calls from me in the span of ten minutes. It's no fun being the fiend-iest, fiend in Fiendsville.

When I couldn't get regular blow, I would go to Hollywood and try to find crack from the street dealers. My friends and I called it "Rock Hunting." What an adventure that was! Getting robbed, buying fake drugs, getting punched in the face, having a weathered prostitute blow crack smoke directly into my mouth as she grabbed my crotch are just a few of my fondest memories of those nights. One of the more notable experiences was the time I almost got stabbed.

I went to the parking lot of a doughnut shop that used to be on the corner of Highland and Santa Monica. That was a hotspot for all kinds of rotten shit. I parked my car and surveilled the scene. A guy parked in a dark corner of the lot had customers coming and going from his car window. I knew that was my dude. I walked up and asked him for a couple of "dubs." That's forty dollars' worth of rock cocaine. He handed me a little baggie that I began to inspect. Me, thinking I was some sort of crack sommelier, tasted one of the rocks and said, "Are you sure this isn't aspirin?" I don't know why I said it, but I did. I wanted to seem streetwise, I guess.

My man took offense to my appraisal of his product and opened his car door with a swift push, knocking me back a little. He then grabbed a flathead screwdriver that was in the door panel of his car and firmly put it into my ribs. It would have broken skin if I weren't wearing a leather jacket. He got in my face close enough to where I could feel his breath and said, "Don't you tell me my shits aspirin, motherfucker!" and he snatched the forty dollars out of my hand, got back in his car, and took off.

I returned to my car in a state of disbelief. The girl I was with who watched the whole thing said, "What the fuck just happened?!"

"I almost got stabbed!" I declare with a nervous chuckle. I brushed it off, and we continued through Hollywood and enjoyed the rest of our night/morning, occasionally laughing about what had happened. Oh, and I was wrong. It was indeed legitimate crack.

I thought how absurdly surreal this whole situation was. The entire chain of events was insane. Just a day prior, I was released from county jail. I've forgotten what offense it was for that time, but I'm not a hardened criminal nor an actual drug addict. Yet, here I am, fresh out of lock-up, still driving drunk on a suspended license (the same crimes that put me in jail in the first place), almost getting stabbed in a parking lot trying to buy crack! *Who the fuck am I?!* But even after assessing what just happened, I still never thought this was problematic. It was just another crazy night. Laugh it off; on to the next.

Last Call, Stupid

After sampling a few treats in the world of hard drugs, I wanted to try them all. I'd get high on whatever was available or offered to me—meth, heroin, acid, ecstasy, mescaline, Adderall, Oxycontin... I did not discriminate. I snorted, swallowed, and smoked just about everything under the sun. I even intravenously shot up cocaine a couple of times (pot and shrooms were also on the menu, but I don't consider them "dangerous narcotics".) I welcomed anything and everything after I had a few drinks. Although I danced with some of the most viciously addictive substances, I never developed a dependency on any narcotic, nor did I ever do them without drinking. I never sold property or stole anything for drugs. It was strictly recreational. I had seen too many friends go down terrible roads, and some even die from addictions. Alcohol was my full-time job. Drugs were just a hobby.

Speed, meth, crystal, whatever you want to call it was too intense for me. Sure, I'd do it if I were feeling particularly desperate, and it was the only thing available, but I never sought it out. It made me feel superhuman for the first few hours, but then it didn't fucking stop. Methamphetamine doesn't come with an off switch. Once ingested, you better buckle up because it's taking you on a long ride. Have you ever walked out of a dark, windowless club at 10 a.m. after nearly twelve hours of partying into the unfathomably bright, hot light of day? It's an inexplicably advanced level of regretting your choices.

In another clip from my highlight reel, one night when I was coming home from a night of drinking, I pulled up to my parent's house around 2:00 in the morning and saw my old neighbor friend, turned tweaker outside. I was a little liquored up and had to be at work in a couple of hours, so I had the brilliant idea of asking him if he had a bump or two he could spare to sharpen me up for my shift. He said, "I sure do!"

I went into his house and started doing lines with him. My experience with crystal meth before this was limited. I had done it only once in San Francisco and liked it. In retrospect, it was because I did a small amount. I was used to cocaine, which you can do a line every twenty minutes. That was part of the fun. Crystal, on the other hand, is not the same. A little dab is all you need to get you going, like how one drop of Ghost Pepper extract will enrage an entire pot of chili. Speed is also painful to snort. There's a reason some people call it "Glass."

After inhaling a few uncomfortable lines with my old buddy, I went home and got ready for work. I was feeling way too tweaked out to handle the morning rush of a coffee shop, so I thought I'd even out by drinking more. I consumed a couple of beers on my drive to work. That wasn't the best idea. When I started my shift, I felt utterly scrambled. My mind and heart rate were going at a thousand miles per hour from the meth, but I was slurring my words and didn't have all my motor skills from the alcohol. It was like a dream when you're trying to run or punch someone, but you feel like you're in slow motion. It was a truly bizarre experience.

On my break, I decided making a giant, supercharged whippet out of one of the whipped cream canisters would be a good choice. A few of my coworkers would do this all the time, but given my state, it probably wasn't my best idea. I took an empty whipped cream container, filled it with several nitrous oxide charges, and huffed it in one giant inhale. The next thing I knew, I was on the floor, getting shaken awake by my manager. The massive hit of noz I took caused me to faint, and on my way to the ground, my head smashed into the dish sanitizer. I was sent home, yet surprisingly not fired. (Remember when I said how ridiculous doing noz was in the previous chapter? This is how alcohol changes you, kids.)

I was up for two days straight after that. The feeling of being so completely exhausted but unable to sleep is excruciating. I got to the point where I was seeing shadow figures walking around my room. I also got the shakes and bouts of nausea as the drug left my body. It was a lesson hard learned, but it didn't stop me from doing it again.

I also had some adverse reactions to crack a couple of times. Crack! Who would have thought that could lead to unpleasantness? There were times I got cold sweats, nausea, and uncontrollable shaking when I was coming down. Once, I had a panic attack so bad I assumed it was the end for me. It was an early Saturday afternoon that was preceded by a night of hard drugs and heavy drinking. I felt like my usual hungover self for that day and time when suddenly my heart started to race so fast, I thought it would burst. I began to sweat, and my vision got cloudy and tunneled. My breath was shallow and rapid. It scared me to the point that I grabbed my phone and had 911 ready to dial. It felt like my life was flashing before my eyes.

Scared of how much an ambulance would cost, I instead decided to walk to the fire station a couple of blocks down the street. The whole time, I had my phone in hand, ready to call emergency services if needed. My heart rate calmed down once I was outside in fresh air, and I could take deeper breaths as I made my way down the street. Unbeknownst to me, getting outdoors and walking is one of the strategies to mitigate the symptoms of a panic attack. It was a terrifying experience, but not enough to keep me from doing drugs again. I'd only suffer one more panic attack of that magnitude several years later in Las Vegas. Cocaine being the common denominator to both experiences.

My relationship with ecstasy—E, X, Molly, or whatever you'd like to call it—lasted for a couple of years. I would wind up abusing it a little too much and eventually stopped. The first time dropping a pill is unexplainable. My entire body buzzed. It enhanced every sense I had by a thousand percent. The most striking effect was my sense of well-being for myself and others. I wanted to comfort the whole of humanity, give it a hug and a kiss, and say, "You're all right… Everything is love and beauty."

I started going to underground, jungle, drum & bass warehouse parties. Everybody was rolling (on ecstasy). The sense of community, love, and good vibes was infectious. Cuddling up next to ten or twenty people in an "E puddle" felt so cozy and meaningful. For someone like me at that time in my life, to have such a positive feeling, even for a few hours, was remarkable. Methylenedioxymethamphetamine, or MDMA, was used by psychiatric professionals for decades before the Feds decided it was a Schedule One narcotic. The effect of the drug would encourage participants to be more receptive to treatment by making them more vulnerable and letting their guard down to share their feelings, expanding their consciousness. (Thankfully, MDMA and many other psychedelics are on their way to being legalized because of the overwhelming data supporting their benefits for mental health.)

MDMA works by flooding your brain with serotonin and oxytocin. The downside of that is it depletes your brain of those chemicals for days after. I was taking two to four pills every weekend for two years. I was highly prone to depression back then, which made for a very dark, terrifying come down that would sometimes last a week or until I dropped my next pill. After a few annihilatory hangovers, I decided I had had enough and quit cold turkey. The pills I was taking weren't the pure pharmaceutical variety. The street chemists created their own versions with all kinds of different goodies to give it a little more kick, including cocaine, meth, LSD... Some of my favorite pills were mixed with heroin and mescaline. I believe, in the long run, I got something positive and vital from MDMA. It allowed me to experience a profound gratitude and appreciation for people and life itself. It opened a window in my consciousness to which I will forever have access.

Out of all the various drugs I tried, cocaine was my drug of choice when I was drinking. Not so much for the feeling but for the utility. A few of my bandmates affectionately referred to coke as "survival kit" for its ability to sober you up and get you through the night. It allowed me to drink a hell of a lot more and keep the party going, sometimes leading to near-alcohol poisoning. There were a few times I drank way more than I should have because of coke and became unresponsive to the point where my friends almost called an ambulance. Those were the instances where I could sense legitimate concern from them, but instead of seeing it as a sign, I just shrugged it off. The remorse and shame I felt from those situations never translated to cutting back. A crushing cocaine and whiskey hangover wasn't enough to keep me from alcohol. The feeling would only last until my next beer was in hand. Repentance from drinking was only absolved by more drinking.

Throughout my whole life, I've always had a darkness in me, but it really started to manifest when I began to drink. Alcohol, at first, makes everything fun and carefree, but then it starts to change into a monster. When I was drunk and alone, I would take my thoughts and emotions out on myself. I had some spells of self-mutilation throughout my twenties that started slow but ramped up over time.

My usual outlet was taking a razor blade to myself. I enjoyed the look of the blood and the feeling and sound of my flesh ripping open. There was an odd sense of pleasure I'd get from it. I'd also twist up wire coat hangers into various shapes and letters, heat it until it was red hot, and brand myself. I'd pierce safety pins just about anywhere on my body, including my nipples, scrotum, and throat. Sometimes, I'd do it in front of people just to get a rise out of them. I know now these were emotional problems that manifested themselves in peculiar ways, but back then, I just thought I liked doing it.

I never tried to commit suicide by cutting; however, one evening, I got too aggressive and had to call a friend over because I was afraid I had gone too far. I never flaunted my scars or did it for attention. I'd try to hide my cuts from friends and family the best I could. I've since covered my scars with tattoos, but they are still visible if you look close enough. There's an art form in Japan called "Kintsugi". When something breaks, like a cup or vase, it is repaired using melted gold to mend the pieces back together, making it stronger, more beautiful, and unique. That's how I see my scars now.

I wouldn't say I ever tried to end it all in a traditional sense, but I did intentionally put myself in positions where my life was in severe jeopardy. A couple of times, I did "suicide runs" in my car. I read about it in Mary Tyler Moore's autobiography. She described how she would get hammered and race down streets at high rates of speed without stopping for any lights or stop signs. Who would have thought I'd be inspired to do dangerous suicidal activities from America's sweetheart? I'm immensely grateful that I never hurt or killed anybody doing that. If you want to harm or destroy yourself, that's one thing, but don't take anybody else with you.

I played Russian roulette with a live round once. That was a terrifying experience. I was in a very dark, drunken state when I grabbed one of my father's 357 magnum revolvers, loaded one round in the chamber, and put it in my mouth. I can still feel and taste the cold iron of the barrel when I think about it. With tears streaming down my face, I spun the cylinder and pulled the trigger. Hearing the clack of the hammer puts things in perspective real quick. It's like when you flip a coin for something. It'll reveal your true preference for the desired outcome no matter how it lands. I still wonder if I would have heard the bang if the gun had gone off.

I once tried sitting in a closed garage in my car with the engine running, but that only gave me a headache. I had seen this method done in movies but wasn't sure if it actually worked. The garage was large, and I wasn't confident it would do the trick, but my heart and spirit were drunk and defeated that night, and I didn't want to wake up to face another miserable day. I pulled in, shut the door, and fell asleep, hoping for the worst. I was passed out in my idling car for several hours just to wake up with a worse-than-usual dizzy hangover.

All this dark madness was fueled by alcohol. I never attempted anything so drastic and violent when I was sober. Sure, I had depression and harmful thoughts, but I would not have acted upon any of them if it weren't for the drinking. Alcohol kept my mood and emotions in a chaotic spin cycle. It never let me leave its grasp. It was my abusive partner that I kept running back to, no matter how bad it hurt me. The first time I ever sought professional mental health was in my mid-twenties at the urging of my friend, Lindsay. She had experience with therapy and psychologists, knew how despondent I could get, and almost begged me to go. Grateful for the compassion, I took her advice and saw a psychologist and psychiatrist. I didn't go very long, but I got a lot out of the experience. I was prescribed an antidepressant, which I took for a few months until I decided ecstasy was a better route. Of course, you know what they say about hindsight, right?

No matter how much trouble I got in, it wasn't a deterrent. I still drove drunk and unlicensed regularly. There were a few times I got pulled over, driving very illegally, but the DUI gods showed mercy on me. One night, around 2:00 a.m., I was driving home on side streets, trying to avoid detection, when a cop started trailing me. My heart began to pound, and my stomach twisted into a knot. I had expired registration tags, a suspended license, an open container in the car, and, to top it all off, a gram of coke on me. I already had two DUIs. A third would have been a felony and some real time in jail. When the police turned their lights on, I thought I was downright fucked.

As I was pulling over, I grabbed the little baggie of cocaine and tried to swallow it with no luck. I couldn't choke down the sharp little corners of the plastic. As the cops approached, I placed the bag between my upper gum and cheek in the back of my mouth. They had me get out of the car and had their usual questions. The officer I spoke to was no more than three feet away from my face. I kept my sentences short, and when I could, I just nodded or shook my head with "Uh huh" and "Uh uh" to limit the movement of my mouth. He then asked if he could search my car, which I consented to. He had me sit in the back of their squad vehicle while they tore apart my car. My oral sleight-of-hand trick with the baggie worked.

When I was in the back of their cruiser, I desperately tried again to swallow the bag of blow. This little goddamn sack just didn't want to slide down my throat. So, I finally started to chew on it, eating all the cocaine. From there, I held the bag with my teeth and pulled it apart with my fingers, ripping it into little pieces. I gave up trying to swallow it, so I started forcing the little bits of baggie behind the plastic door panel. I was able to hide the whole thing in their car. I wonder if they ever found it.

After they ransacked my vehicle, the officers came back to let me out. I'm assuming they were looking for something more serious. One of them said, "Okay, Mr. Josh, I know this isn't your first rodeo. I'm going to let you go, but you'll leave the car parked where it is for the night, and you can come get it tomorrow." I was absolutely stunned.

Without skipping a beat, I said, "You got it! I'll walk home from here!" I shook his hand and thanked him several times.

They got back in their car and drove off. I stood there for a minute, still shaking from fear, shock, and all the cocaine I just ate. I couldn't believe my luck. I grabbed the rest of my twelve-pack, the already opened can of beer in the center console, and started the walk back home. I drank the rest of my twelver along the way, in a state of euphoric disbelief.

There were countless times I put myself in jeopardy while drunk. Not just from law enforcement, but by simply not giving a fuck about my surroundings and personal safety. Out of all the shady drug deals I was a part of, I'm lucky to have escaped relatively unscathed. Getting in the back seat of cars with gang members in the hopes they're going to sell you drugs and not rob or kill you is a real leap of faith. If it wasn't intentionally self-inflicted, general drunken stupidity also inflicted injuries. Rolling ankles, hitting my head, falling down, fracturing bones, waking up with mystery bruises–Intoxicated carelessness was detrimental to my physical health. There were a lot of mornings when I woke up in extreme pain and had no recollection of what had happened. There were quite a few funny predicaments as well.

One evening, my friend Boogie and I met some people at a bar and later went to their West LA house. After a couple of hours, the party died down, and Boogie went into a bedroom with a girl he met, leaving me alone in the living room. I didn't want to sit in this strange house by myself, so I decided to sit in my car and wait for him to come out. He had driven to the party, and I forgot he still had my car keys. Locked out, I laid on the grassy sidewalk beside my car and dozed off.

I woke up about an hour later, with no friend in sight. I walked back to the house and was met by a *now*-locked front door. I figured I must have locked it behind me when I left. The lights were off in the living room, so I couldn't make anything out by looking through the window. I tapped the glass several times hoping someone would hear me, but to no avail. I then went around to the side of the house where I had to scale a fence to get into the backyard to see if a back door was open. As luck would have it, the back kitchen door was unlocked.

When I entered the home, my boots made the old wooden floors creek and thud. No matter how lightly I tried to walk, I was causing a racket. I slowly descended the dark hallway with heavy Doc Marten footsteps whispering my friend's name, "Boogie...Boogie...where are you, Boogie?" I put my ear up to all the closed doors and couldn't hear anybody stirring around. I got to the end of the hallway and back to the living room, where I was presented with something I was not prepared for. As I looked around, something seemed off. The pictures on the wall looked different. I didn't recognize the couch. I remembered there being a coffee table. Everything in the room was completely different! I was in the wrong goddamn house!

After waking up from my nap on the sidewalk, I had miscalculated where the party was by a few houses. Once my initial shock and horror of being an unwitting cat burglar subsided, I swiftly ran to the front door, unlocked the deadbolt, relocked the doorknob, shut the door behind me, and got the fuck out of there. The fact that the homeowners didn't kill me or call the cops is pure luck.

If anybody reading this remembers hearing heavy footsteps in their hallway and a sad, desperate voice whispering, "Boogie...Boogie!" in the middle of the night, it was me. My bad.

ON AND ON

On the road that we all come and go on, down near the graves of the slaves and babes. we laugh as we pass, my lead foot hits the gas, we got our youthful arrogance, but you know that just won't last. And the moonlight glows like our young souls, lovely self-indulgence dolls, ignorant of control. We're soaking up the sin, we lick our lips with a grin, then we sink into a drink and let the night begin.

On and on we go

We create, we make love from hate, yet we laugh at all the losers who just sit and wait. Because what we realize with our eyes to the sky, there's no reason to be circumscribed with the threat of our demise. With a bullet we speed down the same street, singing the same old songs, keeping the beat with our feet. And we know if we go down this road too slow, regret is imminent, so to the far left lane we go.

On and on we go

Limits don't exist, If there's no care, there's no risk

Take a ride with your best disguise on, live the lie of your lonely life

I know the lies and the disguise of the barflies, as the poison penetrates my blood, I see with new eyes. I know I'm no better, and I couldn't get worse. I am saturated sovereign, prophesizing with a slurred verse. At a furious pace, I move on with haste, I'm gonna set the night on fire until it turns into a court case. I've never been alive, and so how can I die? All the bridges will be burned as I speed on by.

On and on we go

Take a sip of the blood you thrive on, keep on running until you're out of life

Crime & Consequence

"I don't like jail, they got the wrong kind of bars in there."

~ Charles Bukowski

I started getting into trouble with the law soon after I began drinking. I technically got two DUIs (driving under the influence) before I was twenty-one, but one of them was dismissed by the police department. Over the years, I'd later get two more, along with a couple of driving on a suspended license convictions and probation violations that stemmed from the DUIs. Not to mention several near misses that could have led to felonies. I've spent fifty or so days in jail collectively over the years. I even had the police come to my house once and arrest me right in front of my girlfriend just minutes post-coitus. Since I answered the door wearing only a robe, the cops let her grab some clothes to put on me. She chose a pair of purple swim trunks, a T-shirt with stains on it, and flip-flops. I got to wear that outfit in jail all weekend and in front of the judge the following Monday.

I shockingly only got one drunk and disorderly charge in my twenty-year-long party life. There was a span of about seven years where I always had a court date looming in my future. All my trouble came from conflating alcohol with a motor vehicle. I never cared or took any of it seriously. I viewed it as part of the game, like getting a penalty in hockey. For example, I was arrested for my second DUI a few weeks before my twenty-first birthday. I was pulled over after rolling a stop sign half a block from my house. The cop let me park my car at home before he took me to the station. When you get a DUI, they confiscate your physical driver's license. My first thought was *without an ID, I won't be able to do shit on my twenty-first. Fuck that!* So, as I was sitting in the Glendale drunk tank, I concocted a plan.

I hopped on a bus and returned to my house when I was released at 6:00 a.m. I ran inside, grabbed some beers, got in my car, and drove straight to the DMV. I drank in their parking lot until it opened. As soon as they unlocked their doors, I staggered in and got my picture taken for a regular identification card. The new ID, dawning a slightly buzzed, fresh-out-of-jail picture of me, arrived a couple of days before my birthday. My master plan had come off without a hitch!

Shortly after that incident, I got caught driving on a suspended license. The court had suspended it for a few months and put me on summary probation for the DUI. But I wasn't going to let that stop me from driving. Have you tried getting around on the Metro system in LA? Forget it! Back then, driving on a suspension came with a mandatory thirty days in jail. Men's Central in downtown LA is notoriously violent with famously abusive deputies. I was just a skinny twenty-one-year-old, punk kid when the court ordered me to surrender myself into custody. My nerves were officially rattled.

The week before my surrender date, I started to get scared. Thirty days was a long time! In a drunken fit of inspiration, I decided I would run. I'd be a dangerous fugitive, living the rest of my days on the lamb. I packed my shit, grabbed a Thomas Guide (for all you youngsters, a Thomas Guide is a book of road maps. We used it in the Palaeolithic era, before GPS), and took off.

My girlfriend at the time was in college in Chico, California. That was nearly 500 miles north of where I was. I thought that'd be the perfect place to hide from the long arm of the law. My first stop was a grocery store. I would need money, beer, and cigarettes for my eight-hour drive. There weren't ATMs back then, so the only way to get cash when the banks were closed was to write a personal check at the store. I was so drunk I had to squint one eye as I tried to fill out the check. The cashier stepped in to help me. I got my rations and cash, hopped in my car, and drove northbound. I don't remember any of that eight-hour drive.

It only took a couple of days to see the gaping holes in my plan. My brilliant drunk epiphany didn't hold up under the sober light of day. I headed back home, petrified that I had to go to jail. I managed to make it back in time for my court date. My life as a dangerous evader of justice had finally come to an end. I turned myself in and got my first dose of life behind bars. The most notable souvenir I would take from it would be fearlessness. I was no longer afraid of jail. It was a P.O.W. medal I could proudly display on my rockstar uniform. It would be the first of many trips I would take over the next several years.

My second DUI was a little more chaotic. It was a couple of years after the first. The iPod had just come out. (If you remember when that happened, it was fucking magical!) I just wanted to sit in my car and listen to music. I was parked in front of my house and had a pack of cigarettes, some beers, and a bottle of Captain

Morgan. I had no reason to drive anywhere but apparently, my blackout-drunk self, or perhaps the captain, had places to go.

I woke up in Glendale jail with an insane hangover. My head was throbbing like my heart was beating inside my skull. My body ached as though I had been in a MMA fight. I had bruises in the shape of fingers on both my arms and red marks on my wrist. There was a medical mask in my pants pocket. Wet pants, I might add. What the fuck happened?

After I processed out, I hopped on that same public chariot that had taken me back home from jail once before. This time felt different. Sure, I had been blackout drunk countless times, but with no real serious repercussions other than pissing some people off, in my pants, or wherever I was sleeping. Making an ass out of myself was a frequent thing, one of my signature specialties. I knew I fucked up good this time. I was fighting back tears on the bus as I made my way home. My head had a low, humming vibration that was driving me nauseous. My vision was unfocused and scrambled as I rested my forehead against the bus window, watching all the colors blur and trail off as we drove on. When I got to my house, I realized my car was gone. This was a bad omen.

I was in a total fog. I had no clue what had happened. My car was in a police impound lot. My mother took me there and loaned me the money to get my car out. It was intact, except for a flat tire and some scrapes on the side. Seeing the damage didn't resurrect any memories. I was still utterly oblivious to what had happened.

I was a nervous wreck when I went to court a month later. I knew I was facing stiffer consequences this time. I opted to speak to a public defender about my case. I was assigned a younger lawyer sporting a goatee and a braided ponytail that went halfway down his back. He defended the public by day and played bass in a metal band by night. He approached me with a concerned "What the fuck have you done?" look on his face. "Hello, sir, what do you remember from that night?" That's never a good thing to hear.

When I told him, "Not much," he opened his folder and put a painfully bright light on the darkness of my memory. The cops found me in my car with my pants down, just a few houses from my own. I had flattened my tire when I hit the curb, coming to rest in my neighbor's bushes. The cops had brought me to a hospital to take my blood because I could not stand on my own, let alone use a breathalyzer. I started fighting with the officers, so they wrestled me into a wheelchair, handcuffed my wrists to the armrests, and tied my legs back. Completely restrained, I resorted to my last act of defiance and tried spitting on them. They had to gag me with the medical mask. It explained the pain and bruises all over my body when I woke up in jail. The mask in my pocket was a souvenir. After he read the report back to me, I had flashes of struggling with the cops, but that was about it.

Holy fucking shit! I did that?! How unhinged have I become? There have been a lot of moments in my life where I felt like I was in some terrible, sometimes strangely beautiful, absurd movie. It was like I was watching from some other vantage point, eating popcorn, thinking, *what the fuck is this guy gonna do next?!* I had a range of emotions coursing through me after being enlightened of my misdeeds: embarrassment, shame, and a pinch of feeling like a badass for fighting with the police.

The fear of whatever penalty I would receive was significantly diminished because I was no longer afraid of jail. I knew what to expect. Fines and classes are only inconveniences. Not at any point during all of this did I once think about quitting alcohol. Drinking wasn't the problem–getting caught was. The court had even put in my probation terms that I would be in violation if I were caught drinking (in any capacity) or seen around liquor stores or bars. I thought that was ridiculous and unenforceable. After receiving my sentence, I carried on as if nothing had happened, getting in my car with expired tags and driving away from the courthouse without a license.

I earned my third (technically fourth) DUI in 2009 when I was thirty-two years old, and it would wind up being my harshest punishment to date. I made the mistake of driving in Orange County after a couple of beers. (Orange County borders LA County to the south.) The OC operates differently than LA regarding crime and punishment, especially with DUIs.

The circumstances of the arrest were just plain dumb. I had pulled over to take a picture of a Claim Jumper restaurant. Long story short, I needed the picture to send to a friend to win a bet. There weren't many cars on the street, and I pulled over out of the way of traffic. I wasn't stopped more than thirty seconds before the police were behind me with their lights on. Unbeknownst to me, I was in a bus-only zone, and they came to investigate. They did their whole song and dance, taking me out of my car, making me do all their tests, and finally having me blow into a breathalyzer. I had blown just one-tenth of a point over the limit.

Thirty days later I show up to court, thinking it will be the same scenario I'm used to. I thought I'd be getting a first-offender conviction because my other two DUIs were so old—no such luck. One was just two months shy of falling off my record, thus making me eligible for the much stiffer second-offender sentencing. I knew how that process went, so I didn't bother talking to a public defender. When I approached the bench, the prosecuting DA looked at me like a cheetah eyeballing a three-legged gazelle. When the judge asked her to proceed with her recommendations, my jaw just about hit the floor. As if the fines, probation, classes, and car interlock weren't enough, I got forty-five days in jail to boot.

Completely stunned, I asked the judge if I could talk to a lawyer before I accepted the terms. There was a public defender right next to me saying that my blood alcohol level was so low (.09) that they could probably get a much lesser sentence. The judge said, "Okay. We'll see you back here in a couple of weeks." I was relieved for a second until immediately after that, he added, "Ballif," as he pointed at me. The deputy walked up and handcuffed me right in front of the packed courtroom.

What the fuck is happening! I said inside my head. This type of thing doesn't happen in LA. Every time I've received a future court date, I've been let go on my own recognizance until the specified date. Not only did I not have bail, it was the Wednesday before Thanksgiving, meaning I would have been held in a holding tank at least until the following Monday. There was no way I could do that, so I swallowed the absurdly harsh sentence without a fight. The judge let me surrender for the forty-five-day jail sentence after the holidays in early January.

Drug addicts will always tell you the first time is the best. I don't know if that sentiment applies to going to jail. My first time was terrifying, but it got easier with each trip. I never took incarceration as the wake-up call it's supposed to be. It's part of the game I was playing; sometimes you pull the go directly to jail card. No big deal. My intention is not to boast about a hard, thuggish street life; Martha Stewart has done more time than me. I won't be glorifying my time on *the inside* or claiming any gang affiliations... I was drunk and had traffic tickets.

Due to overcrowding in LA county detention facilities, non-violent, minor offenses, sometimes don't serve any time at all. I didn't even get processed on a couple of occasions; I walked in and walked out as time served. Twice, they put me on work release. That's when they assign you a community service type of job for X amount of days. The first time I did that, I cleaned up around the offices where the deputies worked at the jail, and another time, I had to clean up after the police horses near Griffith Park.

My first trip to county jail was due to driving on a suspended license. That carries a thirty-day mandatory sentence. At the same time, I violated the probation from the DUI that caused my license to be suspended in the first place, which tacks on additional time. When I turned myself in on the surrender date given to me, I remember my dad dropping me off at the Glendale court and saying, "Well... good luck." When I appeared before the judge he ordered the bailiff to cuff me and take me to the back holding tank, a windowless concrete room, about twenty by twenty, with a bench that lined the walls. It was filled with ten to fifteen other guys who were either bussed in from county jail or had turned themselves in, like myself. This was the beginning of my journey into the bowels of the American justice system.

With a sharp, loud buzzing sound, the door made a clack as it unlocked. A burst of hot air pushed its way out of the cell. I was twenty-one, pale as a ghost, and thin as a rail. I didn't have the presence of a street thug. The few tattoos that adorned my flesh were not of the tough-guy variety. The other guys in the tank were older, rougher, and at least seemed to have more experience in this jail business than me. It felt like an awkward first day of school, except everyone was an angry criminal. I was scared and profoundly alone. There was no one to call, hug, or have my back. There was nothing familiar or consoling here. It was a stunning realization.

I kept to myself in the tank. It wasn't difficult. There were the obligatory "what are you in for" chats, but those didn't last long. There was a homeless fellow in the corner who seemed to be having withdrawals from whatever poison he fancied. The stench of body odor, anger, and frustration was pungent. The heat from all the bodies in the tiny room coaxed the sweat from my pores. We all just sat and waited for hours until the Los Angeles County Sheriff's bus came to whisk us away to the county jail downtown—the Twin Towers. The reputation of this venue was no secret to me. I was petrified to make this next stop on my journey.

Suddenly, the loud buzz and twisting of the lock shook us out of our angry boredom. Four deputies entered the cell, yelling at everyone to line up against the wall. One of them was carrying a chain with shackles attached to it. "Line up, ladies," he smugly uttered as we formed a line. They paired us up, shoulder to shoulder, and then chained us together in a line. It seemed everybody knew this but me because the disturbed homeless man was the only one left to get partnered up with. When they put the restraints on us, he started to pull and jerk around while shrieking with impressive intensity. In LA, where homelessness is rampant, seeing a mentally ill person behaving strangely on the street is easy to dismiss because it's so common—when that person is tethered to you by a short chain, you get a whole new appreciation for that individual's problems.

The guy ahead of me was a stocky Latino gent with a shaved head that was wholly inked up with various numbers and initials, signifying the neighborhood where he was from. He turned around, looked at me, and said, "You better handle that, fool." There was nothing casual about the delivery of his request; it was my first test. Whenever the homeless man tried to pull away, I kept a firm hold on the chain so he didn't take me with him. He made a quick move as if he were going to run somewhere, tightening the slack that bound us. I grabbed the chain and yanked it as hard as I could, bringing me face to face with him. I looked straight into his eyes and, as harsh and menacing as I could, barked, "Calm the fuck down," as I gave the chain another hard pull. I meant business. If I was going down, I'd go down swinging. I had scared adrenaline flowing through my veins, making my whole body hum with nervous excitement, hoping that everyone was buying the tough, alpha male bullshit I was selling. It seemed to be working as the COs (correctional officers) escorted us outside.

If you thought it wasn't possible to make a bus ride worse than Greyhound, the LA County Sheriffs sure the fuck figured it out. It's black and white and the size of a regular school bus. Inside are metal plates over the windows leaving only a little slit to see out of. The bus drives to various courthouses around LA to pick up other troublemakers with court dates. The final destination is the Twin Towers Correctional Facility on Bauchet Street.

When we arrived, a giant ominous gate slowly opened letting the bus into the inmate receiving area. Here, we are unchained and put into a little room. It would be one of several hot, gross holding cells I'd occupy during my stay. After about an hour, we were funneled into another room where four belligerent deputies came to welcome us by screaming obscenities and ordering us to put our faces against the wall. Whoever attempted to look at what was happening got their face mushed back into the concrete bricks. We were told to disrobe and put our clothes by our feet. LA County jail was notorious for police brutality back then. It lived up to the stories. The officers wanted us to know we no longer had any rights. Message received! This first interaction inside the towers was so over the top, that if you were to see it in a movie, you wouldn't believe it was realistic. Truth is often more horrifying and grotesque than fiction.

After being stripped of our clothes and identity, the deputies shouted, "Get in line, nuts to butts!" having us form a tight line as we were herded into another room to get our new outfits, which looked like blue medical scrubs, a.k.a. the county blues. The black shoes they provide are like a shitty version of Vans slip-ons. Getting a pair in good condition was a coveted prize. If you are gay or trans, need medication, are in a gang, or are not identifiable as Black, White, or Hispanic, you are given different colored clothing and separated from the other animals.

With our new outfits and wristbands with inmate numbers, we were bounced around from room to room for over twenty hours before we got our sleeping accommodations. The cells that we were rotated through are small and standing room only. If you got a bench seat, you were lucky. When I dozed off for a minute, I found myself on the wrong side of a deputy's boot. During the course of this sleepless, almost day-long period, we were given sack lunches that included a juice box, some cookies, and a sandwich that consisted of a hamburger bun and some very suspicious-looking bologna.

Once I entered my assigned cell block, a grizzled, leathery-looking skinhead immediately waved me over. He gave me my "fish kit," which included a toothbrush, toothpaste, soap, and a razor for shaving. He informed me of all the unwritten rules and codes of conduct the inmates follow. The Whites were known as "Woods." It doesn't matter if you're a skinhead or just a regular Joe, if you're caucasian, you have to hang out with the Caucasians. The Hispanics separated themselves into two categories: Southsiders and Piasanos. The Southsiders were usually younger street criminals, and the Piasanos were typically unaffiliated, working-class, older gentlemen. The Black guys were just "The Blacks." Asians and Middle Eastern or "non-white whites" are completely separated from the general population.

Each group had a "rep". They were like the spokesperson for each demographic. If tension built up between groups, they would discuss it before any immediate altercation occurred. Spontaneous fights between races happened, but the reps usually stopped it quickly and made decisions on when and where it should be handled before a riot broke out. Inner-race conflicts were not regulated with the same protocol. If you didn't play by the rules, your team would sort you out and engage in disciplinary action. I saw this happen several times to people who couldn't wrap their heads around their new environment and resisted adaptation. They needed a little roughing up to help them understand their predicament with more clarity.

The entire dorm was segregated. Every group had their own tables, toilets, and phones, and would take turns using the showers. I had never seen or heard of anything like it. Growing up in LA, I was going to school and hanging out with all different kinds of people, but seeing blatant racism like this was blindsiding. Since this was pre-internet and before endless TV channels showing prison documentaries, my knowledge of jail was also limited. The whole environment was so volatile that if you weren't paying attention to every little nuance, you could quickly get into trouble.

It was clear that the COs were the most dangerous because they could do whatever they wanted with complete impunity. When they acted violently or instigative, there was nothing you could do about it without severe consequences. At least if something happened with another inmate, you had a fighting chance.

The only time I had to deal with Nazis before was when they would show up at punk shows and stir up trouble. I even got in a fight with a bunch of them at a gig I played in Victorville once. Now, I was forced to hang out with them. Intelligent conversations in jail are a rare commodity. One of the first guys I talked to was telling me in precise detail about how he blew his wife's head off with a shotgun in their trailer. I don't know if he was telling the truth or not—there seemed to be a lot of tall tales in there—but it made me uncomfortable, nonetheless. Most people in jail are awaiting their trial or on their way to federal prison—I was in there for a trumped-up traffic ticket. That didn't win me a lot of street cred; I could only observe and maintain a low profile to keep myself out of trouble.

Since my crime wasn't serious, my fellow inmates told me I'd probably be released within a day or two. This raised my hopes; I didn't know if I could handle thirty days of the hell I was in. At night a deputy would enter the dorm and call out the names and numbers of the people being released or moved elsewhere. "Roll it up!" Meaning roll up the plastic mattress (if they had given you one) and grab your shit. On my second night, my name and number were called. I was beyond relieved when I heard my name, but it wasn't to go home. I was being moved to a jail called Wayside, or Pitchess Detention Center, in the Santa Clarita Valley. *WHAT THE FUCK?!*

It was back into the maze of holding tanks until a group of us was put on a bus and shipped forty miles north of Downtown LA, which made me more nervous. The facility is nestled near the mountains and looks like a summer camp for degenerates. The dorms had windows, and I felt like I was in nature. The location was farther from home than downtown LA and seemed more isolated, so whenever I used the phone to call my girlfriend or family, I had to fight back tears. I couldn't let anyone see me cry; that would've been bad for my health. But it wasn't just using the phone; I would get teary-eyed if I thought about any part of my real life. So I learned to completely disconnect from myself and focus only on my present situation. This was a tactic I would use repeatedly throughout my life.

I was at Wayside for a few days until they shipped me back to LA. Once there, I began processing out. Much like when I arrived, moving through various holding tanks took almost twenty-four hours until I was freed. They let me out around midnight, and my girlfriend and mother came to pick me up. I demanded we stop at a liquor store so I could get beer and cigarettes. I was only in jail for roughly seven days, but it impacted me for the next several weeks. I witnessed multiple fights and deputies beating people up for seemingly no reason. I watched them rough up the mentally ill and elderly alike. It was an eye-opening experience that showed me how dark the underbelly of humanity can be.

After that first trip, the rest were more manageable. I knew the game and how to compose myself to avoid trouble with the COs and inmates. I was taught that Honey Buns from the commissary could be used as currency, and how to make a little rope from plastic sandwich bags. I was shown how to make a "spread" from Top Ramen and Hot Cheetos. I overcame the embarrassment of having to shower and poo in front of people. I even saw various types of drugs going around, which I didn't understand—the last thing I'd want to be in jail is high on meth or ecstasy. I didn't even drink the coffee that was offered to me because I didn't want the caffeine; sleep was the only respite from the misery I was in.

The last time I went to jail I was in for thirty-two days. In Orange County they make you serve ninety percent of your sentence, so before I turned myself in I drank several beers at a Hooters across the street from the facility. That was the last meal I chose for myself. *What's one more poor decision going to matter at this point, right?* Since I would be locked up for a longer amount of time, I was offered a job in the kitchen to take off a few days of my term. Like the military, all kitchen staff had to be clean-shaven, so I had to shave my head down to the flesh. With my *new do*, I looked like a real mean son-of-a-bitch, straight out of Central Casting for "scary Aryan prison guy." I even told my parents not to visit me because I thought I'd give my mother a heart attack if she saw me.

In addition to the usual politics, there was a "no working out" rule, which meant if you wanted to exercise, you had to get creative to hide from the eyes of the deputies. In the first dorm or "pod" I was in, the only place the COs couldn't see you was in the showers. Each group took turns using the facility to clean themselves–so if you have ever wanted to do naked burpees surrounded by a bunch of soapy Nazi schlongs, I know just the place for you.

Luckily working in the kitchen, someone could keep watch while we curled trash bags filled with water—but making dinner for a few thousand people and cleaning up after is a lot of work. We got to eat better than all the other inmates, but in a way, that made us targets. There was a little window to pass food trays through when you were done eating, and some of these fuckers would push it through as hard as they could, leading to some bloody knuckles and sprained fingers. In the end, the worst thing to happen was that I had to get a tetanus shot after I cut my hand on a commercial meat slicer. The work kept me busy and my mind occupied, so I was grateful for that.

Some nights in the dormitory, we would do what they called a "talent show." After the deputies did the last count, it was lights out, and each group would take turns having someone sing, rap, read a poem, or whatever they wanted to do. When someone was singing, their race no longer mattered. Everyone shut up and respected the singer, whether good or bad. It was a touching, emotionally poignant moment that I hadn't expected, one that made me proud to be a musician, to sing my songs and hear others share theirs. Fittingly, the few songs I sang in front of the literal captive audience were lyrics I wrote about drinking and drug use. Plus the acoustics of the cement floors and metal roof produced an incredible reverb.

The last week there was tough. I was losing my composure and couldn't hide my disdain from the COs. That led to a couple of verbal confrontations, which could have gotten physical, but I was able to de-escalate at the last moment. During my last days, the rep for the Whites processed out, and the other guys wanted me to take over. I was the tallest and maybe the meanest-looking one, but I wanted nothing to do with it. I thought inmates intentionally picking fights with guys who were about to be released just to extend their sentences, so I was trying to keep the lowest profile possible. I left Theo Lacey Facility a somewhat changed man. I had a new appreciation for my life and everyone in it. It also hardened the crust I already had. But, alas, it did not prevent me from doing all the stupid things that got me there in the first place. I was back to my old ways less than a week after this month-long stay.

Last Call, Stupid

Here's to it

I don't want to think about it no more
Don't wanna give it another thought
And I don't wanna see you around here no more
This ain't no longer what I want

But I don't mind the pain
When you're swimming in my veins
And tomorrow's a new day
With new regrets and bills to pay

I don't wanna give you any more time
I ain't got none left to waste
And I don't want you up on my back
I just wanna rinse out the bad taste

But I don't mind the pain
When you're swimming in my brain
And tomorrow's a new day
With new regrets and bills to pay

So here's to you
Here's to me
And better lives and love
Have another
It's on me
Here's to breath and blood

Compromised

In the harsh light of the day
My eyes burn, my hands shake
And I find it hard to breathe

I just drank up all the rent
I no longer wanna be a resident
But I find it hard to leave

I see it in your eyes
The way you compromise
Believing your own lies
When my glass is full
I feel more comfortable
This world is bearable

When my blood is thin
Release serotonin
In the cool light of the moon

I can smile with all the dead
When I get this change inside my head
'Cause I know I'll be there soon

You know I hate convention
And consequence doesn't frighten me
I'll never learn the lessons
Force fed to me

I see it in your eyes
The way you compromise
Believing your own lies
When my glass is full
I feel more comfortable
This world is tolerable

Fail

Fresh out of jail and I got no money
I told a joke, no one thought it was funny
I guess my luck just got the fuck straight out of town
I got drunk and pissed off all of my friends
I never have the means to my ends
But maybe I'm just having one of those days

But it gets no better at all
All I know how to do is fail

My breath smells like a Pabst Blue Ribbon
I've scared off every woman
That's ever gave a goddamn about me
I'm starting to see the age on my skin
I got a bloody nose, my liver's soaked in gin
But I think I'm just down in the dumps today

But it gets no better at all
All I know how to do is fail
No one's proud of me
And no one ever will be

So that's the story and you know it ain't funny
I'm going back to jail and I still have no money
But at least I've got a smile on my face
So mama's keep your kids away from me
I'm no good, and that's clear to see
But maybe I'm just having one of those days

But it never gets better at all
All I know how to do is fail
No one's proud of me
No one ever will be

And that's hard to say
No one's ever gonna be proud of me

The following weekend after my release I drove down to Hermosa Beach to visit my friend. To make my homecoming really special, I bought a twelve-pack of Miller High Life and a rotisserie chicken to celebrate my reintegration into civilian life. I started to drink as much as I usually did, which was a big mistake because my tolerance was far from where it was pre-lock-up. When I left her house, the beers caught up with me quickly, and I got lost on the usually familiar streets trying to get back home.

In my confusion, I made a right-hand turn from the wrong lane, and *BAM*! Red and blue lights appeared in my mirrors. *This can't be happening…this can't be fucking happening!*

I felt nothing as I pulled over–no stomach knots, no stress, just total apathy and defeat. I knew how fucked I was. The officer gave me the usual spiel, explained why he pulled me over, took my ID, and returned to his car. I sat there in disbelief that I was in this situation yet again. I wasn't out of jail for more than six days, and I already got my return ticket to go back. Several desperate measures crossed my mind as I sat and waited for the deputy to return. I contemplated hitting the gas and running, or taking off on foot. I also considered killing myself by taking the seat belt off and crashing full speed into a wall. Anything was better than the reality I was about to face.

The officer returned to my car, handed me my ID, and said, "I'm citing you for turning from the wrong lane. Go ahead and park your car and get a ride from someone else. If I see you driving again tonight, I'm sure you know what will happen."

With a sigh of incomprehensible relief, I said, "Thank you," as if he gave me a second chance at life, and in many ways, he did.

He sat in his cruiser and watched me pull into a parking lot and turn my car off before he left. I'm not sure at what point during that night or perhaps in my whole life I had managed to get a lucky charm the size of a Buick lodged into my ass, but my gratitude for it being there cannot be sufficiently articulated.

After the officer left, my pulse raced and my head spun with disbelief. As I sat in the parking lot, I began to get my bearings and knew where I was and how to get home. It started to rain, and I was too far from my friend's house to walk back. It was before rideshare apps, and it was too late to call anyone to pick me up. I knew I'd be home-free once I got on the freeway because the cops don't patrol there.

Have you been paying attention so far, reader? What do you think I did next? Count my lucky stars, call it a night, and take a nap in my car? Or, do you think I ran for it? If you chose "This fucking idiot is going to press his luck and run," congratulations! You are correct!

Thirty minutes had passed without a trace of the police, so I started my car and drove straight to the highway. I looked in my rearview mirror every few seconds. My heart skipped a beat whenever I saw headlights behind me. My hands were trembling as I white-knuckled the steering wheel. I must have yelled, "HOLY FUCKING SHIT!" a thousand times as I drove down the freeway reeling with adrenaline. It was easy sailing back to my pad, but the night had more excitement in store for me. The exit I took to get to my apartment was one of those slow-down-to-fifteen-miles-per-hour circular off-ramps. Given my panicked state and rain-slicked roads, I misjudged my speed on the ramp I had taken a million times before and crashed right into the side wall. *BANG!* My airbag went off, and my car spun around in a complete three-hundred-sixty-degree turn. *Goddamn it! This can't be happening!*

Dizzy, and completely discombobulated from the impact of the airbag, I thought I may have hit another vehicle. When I realized I had only hit the wall, I knew I had to leave immediately before anybody saw me and called the cops. Despite the airbags deploying and the front of my car a little crunched, it was still running. In my panicked and slightly drunk state, I drove away from the direction of my house and figured I'd park on the street so nobody in my apartment building would see me parking a freshly crashed vehicle. I only made it a couple of blocks from the freeway when it died on me.

I coasted toward the curb as I finally came to a stop. Thinking maybe it just needed a jump, I grabbed my jumper cables from my trunk and waited for a passing car to help me out. (I almost don't want to tell you what happened next because it sounds completely unbelievable, but this is what actually happened.) As I stood next to my car holding jumper cables, in the distance, I saw three different sets of headlights driving down the road toward me. I walked slightly into the street and held up the cables, signaling that I needed a jump. When the first of the three cars got close enough, to my shock and horror, I realized they were all patrol cars.

Was this instant karma for not staying parked after getting the luckiest break of my life? Crashing my car, then having a second encounter with police? As they slowly moved past me, I just smiled and waved them by like nothing was happening. I made eye contact with every single one of them as they slowly made their way down the street, never stopping or rolling down a window. *How many heart attacks can I have in one night?!*

As soon as they were out of sight, I knew I needed to get home before anything else happened. At that point, if an anvil or a piano dropped from the sky and landed on my head, I would not have been surprised. As I put the jumper cables back into the trunk, I noticed I had my street hockey rollerblades with me. What better way to get safely home while drunk on wet streets, than by strapping wheeled boots to my feet? I slid those babies on, and began my trek back home. I collected only minor cuts and bruises on the way. When I got to my apartment, I grabbed a beer from the fridge, sat on my couch, and tried to comprehend the night's insanity. I looked up at the ceiling, unclenched all my muscles, and let out a long, breathy "Fuuuuuuuuuuck."

The Unraveling

"And I'm not sure what the trouble was that started all of this. The reasons have all run away, but the feeling never did. It's not something I'd recommend, but it is one way to live. 'Cause what is simple in the moonlight, by the morning, never is."

~ Conor Oberst

When I was twenty-seven, I had relatively steady employment working at a free weekly newspaper selling ad space in the classified section to mostly prostitutes and psychics. I finally reinstated my driver's license and moved into my first apartment with a girlfriend in North Hollywood. It was the first time I had done something remotely adult. It was more out of necessity than love. We both needed a place to live. She was in a bad roommate situation, and I still lived at my ex-girlfriend's mom's house. My credit score and income were less than desirable to landlords then, and I needed her credentials to get us into an apartment.

We both partied together, but things got rocky when she realized the party never stopped with me. She soon got violently angry every time I drank. When she got mad enough, she would throw whatever was within her arms' reach at me, sometimes leaving holes in the walls. One time I woke up with a message written on a kitchen cabinet in permanent ink that read, "Josh is an asshole when he drinks." Even though I painted over it several times, I could still see it if I looked hard enough.

I found myself hiding in my car and going on walks so I could drink. My frame of mind was she was the problem, not the alcohol. I wasn't going to stop drinking for anybody. I believed it was a permanent fixture in my life; we were a package deal. If she couldn't handle the party anymore, she was the one who needed to leave. My relationship with booze trumped all. It took a little under two years for that relationship to finally crash and burn. Out of the kindness of her heart, she let me keep the apartment. I would spend the next seventeen years in that one-bedroom unit. If those walls could talk, they'd be in therapy.

Alcohol was constantly creating trouble in my romantic relationships, but when I was in my twenties and early thirties, I didn't think much of it or really care. Marriage and kids were the furthest thing from my mind. I had no long-term goals except to be a rockstar and party like one. I honestly didn't think I would live very long, so why bother making plans for a future that probably won't exist? I just wanted to drink all the drinks, do all the drugs, and have all the sex. I had never taken the time to get to know who I actually was. It was as if I was a method actor who had become so enmeshed in the character I created that I lost all touch with the real me.

In my mid-thirties, I met a girl I would be with for five years. We hit it off immediately, so much so that we practically lived together after our first date. She had a pure excitement for simple pleasures that melted my heart. Her childlike sense of enthusiasm veiled her deeper heartbreak of adulthood. It could charm the cockles off even the saltiest of punk rockers. I soon found myself attached to this lovely creature by the hip. We both liked to party and party we did! Our relationship practically revolved around it. After a few amazing years, the thing that brought us together inevitably was the thing that drove us apart. Living in a small, one-bedroom apartment and throwing in a ton of booze, will chip away at the integrity of any relationship. No matter how in love you are, you cannot build a house on a foundation of quicksand. Our talks about marriage and the future soon spun into a downward spiral I didn't have the courage or humility to stop.

It starts slow, a skirmish here, a hissy fit there; it quickly becomes shouting, slamming doors, and being cruel for the sake of being cruel. Whenever I cut a new line of ugliness into the sand, it became the starting point for the next fight, and the altercations just got worse and worse. Ninety-nine percent of our disputes were due to alcohol. It became an uncomfortable, turbulent environment. We were never chemically balanced because we were binge drinking two or three days a week (me more than her). If we were not fighting drunk, we were fighting hungover. Alcohol raised our propensity towards irritability and disproportionate hair-trigger outbursts.

One of the worst feelings was waking up on the couch by myself. That meant something had gone very wrong. Even worse, I had no memory of how vile and belligerent I had been. Hearing about a fight as if I wasn't even there was a profoundly sad, shameful feeling. A couple of mornings, she wasn't even in the apartment anymore. Those days were especially heartbreaking. I had become a grotesque version of Dr. Jekyll and Mr. Hyde, as if I were two different people and had no control over who was in charge. I was finally beginning to see that I wasn't steering the ship anymore, but I didn't know if I could stop it or even wanted it to stop.

The last couple of months together were brutal. I made a feeble attempt to be a better human being, but it was too late; I had fucked this thing up beyond repair. When I realized the relationship was ending, I was gutted. I felt as if I were suffocating–like the atmosphere was somehow constricting around my chest and squeezing the life out of me. I would go through manic fits of crying, rolled up on the floor, begging for the pain to end. I would keep saying, "Please stop. Just please fucking stop!" as if someone were listening to me, or cared. There isn't a word in the English language that could describe the devastation I felt. I was disgusted with how carelessly I treated my girl, who had such a generous, loving heart. I had also become entirely dependent on her. I wasn't just losing my girlfriend/almost fiancée; I had lost everything, including myself.

I was working at my father's auto shop as a technician and office manager, but it wasn't a real job; he was paying me less than minimum wage under the table. The drumming gigs I picked up here and there either paid me in beer or just enough to survive a few days—a month, if I was lucky. I had no form of transportation beyond a bicycle and the Metro. She took most of our friends in the "divorce". My close friends were in different cities, states, or countries. The isolation I found myself in was deafening and disorienting. To make things worse, I had put on forty extra pounds in the last couple of years of our relationship. I suddenly found myself alone, jobless, broke, drunk, and portly. *Portly!* I had become unrecognizable to myself. How had I become this pitiful? It was an excruciating lesson I needed to learn.

The following year was the darkest period of my life. I don't remember a lot of it because I ramped up my drinking quite a bit. The misery I was in was all-encompassing. I started having beers in the morning and throughout the day, whether I was working or not—anything to dull the pain of the emotional hell I had created for myself. To be honest with you, I don't know how I made it out alive. I was too afraid to commit suicide with pills or hanging, which made me feel like a failure even more; if I owned a firearm during those days, I would not be writing this. Even though I grew up with guns around the house, I didn't trust the impulsive, self-destructive behavior I had when I drank. My previous encounter with a weapon years before was enough to scare that idea out of my head.

My first attempt to integrate myself back into society failed miserably. I went to a buddy's house that my Ex and I would frequent. I felt out of place coming alone, like I wasn't welcome. She and I did everything together—a package deal, the "fun party couple." But when Garfunkel shows up to the party without Simon, nobody gives a fuck about just Garfunkel. "Sorry, man". As soon as that sentence left their lips, their eyes would look down and away from mine; as if they were passing my open casket for one last look at the person they used to know.

I drank profusely that afternoon. I vaguely remember doing some coke, but if you've drifted past the point of no return, no amount of cocaine will bring you back to shore. As one of my friends later recalled,

"Dude, I watched you drink a twelve-pack in like, an hour."

I woke up the next day on my couch somehow. I was missing my bicycle and my wallet. *How the fuck did I get home?*

"Hey dude, are my bike and wallet still at your house? How did I get home?"

"Yeah, the bike is still here. I haven't seen a wallet. We put you in an Uber. You were fucking hammered!"

As I opened the front door to leave my apartment, low and behold, there was my wallet on the doormat. Its contents had fallen out, leaving a trail of cards down the hallway. The Uber ride to pick up my bicycle felt long and sad, almost like the bus ride home to my parent's house after my release from jail a decade prior. I felt uncomfortable and helpless.

There's a perverse joy in looking up from the bottom of a hole you've dug to marvel at how deep it has become, admiring your pit of despair. What a fantastically dismal satisfaction. It made me feel closer to Hunter S. and Bukowski, romanticizing my decay and trying to legitimize my self-debasement. *What a crock of shit!* But I was just pointing my finger at everything and everyone being the problem except for myself. I had no idea who I was or what I was capable of doing. I sold myself this lie that I was an incurable useless drunk; so I decided to go as hard as possible from then on. Why not? I had nothing to lose, and the faster I could get to the end of this life, the better.

The next three years were a blur. I hung out with people who were just as self-destructive as myself. If someone didn't want to join the party or couldn't keep up, I moved on; it was that simple. It was a selfish existence. I'm painfully aware now of what an asshole I was, but I couldn't see the forest for the trees at the time. I had moments where I felt ashamed or guilty, but it was more self-pity. Me, me, me!

The only thing I had left was my good ol' pal, alcohol. The patron saint of lowered standards, making the banality of a wretched existence palatable since man discovered the process of fermentation. Drinking was my phantom purpose. The very thing making my life miserable was the only thing that seemed to numb the pain of it. It was the Munchausen mother deliberately making me sick so it could "take care" of me. A bar was always open with another sad soul with whom I could have meaningless conversations for a few hours, temporarily distracting me from my terminal loneliness. Drinking took care of all planning for me—like buying a plane ticket, but I had no clue where I'd end up. Will I wind up snorting cocaine off a butt cheek in Vegas, or on Bourbon Street flashing my dick for beaded necklaces? Maybe I'll wake up in a park with no pants on; let's roll the dice and find out! When I wasn't feeling adventurous, having a few cold ones at home pacified my boredom until I passed out on the couch. Sure, I'm miserable, but it's *my* misery.

When I started thinking that maybe I didn't want to drink anymore, I realized that my entire existence revolved around it. Brick by brick, bottle by bottle, I had been building the prison that kept me a prisoner. I found myself a willing victim; a voluntary slave. I wasn't comfortable with myself or others without my safety blanket. I started to see that every social activity I did with all my friends and family involved alcohol. Winding down from a hard day required libation. There was no part of my life that wasn't corrupted by alcohol.

I was lucky to be in some extraordinary situations, but alcohol kept me from savoring those moments thoroughly. I was never really present, and I often took my good fortune for granted, like becoming an ordained minister to officiate at my best friend's wedding or going on successful domestic and international tours. Instead of remembering how beautiful these experiences were, I think about how I fucked them up or how I disappointed and annoyed the people I was with. I don't regret getting in trouble or all the stupid shit I've done over the years; the times when I was unnecessarily cruel, took advantage of people's kindness or acted like a selfish, obnoxious asshole, are the things that I'm ashamed and remorseful of.

Drinking made everything chaotic, no matter where I was or who I was with. Let me tell you how me and my chaos stumbled into Italy. When I lived in North Hollywood, I was within walking distance of Universal Studios. I would get an annual pass every year, and when I was bored I would get a bottle of vodka, smuggle it into the park, and have myself a day. One time I caught a girl looking in my direction, so I struck up a conversation with her standing in line for the tram tour. She and two of her friends were visiting California from Rome. While on the tram ride, I acted as their secondary tour guide because I knew that place like the back of my hand. After the ride was over, I walked with them for a bit and gave them suggestions of what to check out in LA. I wanted to show them around town myself, but I was a loser with no car or money. I was also pretty buzzed when I met them, and I knew I'd be hammered and no good to anyone in a couple of hours.

I had taken a liking to the first girl I was talking with, so we exchanged social information. In the following months, we started to text each other and have long phone conversations. She often talked about being at a happy hour or some type of club, bar, or show. It seemed like she was always down to party and have a good time, which was a green flag for me because I also loved to party and have a good time—if drinking until you forget about your disfiguring depression counts. Eventually, she invited me to visit Rome and stay with her for a week. She had a two-bedroom apartment in the city, and I could stay in the spare room. The only problem was that I was broke and didn't have money for a plane ticket. But How could I pass up such a fantastic opportunity? After taking inventory of anything of value in my apartment, I decided to sell one of my guitars to my father for the airfare.

I took full advantage of the free alcohol policy on the international flight. I remember starting with a beer and some vodka, and that's about the end of my memory of that thirteen-hour flight. I recall waking up groggy and asking a steward for a beer toward the end of the trip. He gave me a death stare and said sarcastically, "You mean some water." I'll never know what I did, but I did something. I hope it was just my blackout-drunk sleep apnea snoring. My pants were on correctly and dry, so that was a comfort.

It was late in the evening when I staggered off the plane, and I was tired and slightly hungover—not the impression I wanted to make in front of the girl who graciously invited me to stay with her. When I got in her car, the first thing she said was, "You smell like alcohol." "Yes," I said. "It was a long flight!" She asked me if I just wanted to rest or go out, I rallied and said, "Let's go get some drinks!"

At the bar, I ordered a liter of beer, which was not a lot for me, but when she saw the giant German stein, she looked bewildered and said, "That's usually what people order for the table to share." I should have caught the vibe right then and there, but like I said, I hadn't been wholly coherent for twenty years. I was in an elite class of drunkards by then, a world-caliber professional; I could've drank four or five of those and thought I was okay. After a couple of rounds, we went to her place and smoked cigarettes on her balcony. She went to bed before me. I stayed up and drank the rest of her vodka and had a few of her smokes, figuring I'd replace everything I consumed the next day.

BAM! BAM! Two hard knocks on the bedroom door startled me awake. "It's two o'clock!" said an angry Italian voice. The long flight and nonstop drinking had knocked me out. I scrambled out of bed, put myself together, and emerged from the room to greet my angry host. She was a *tad miffed* that I had enjoyed her cigarettes and vodka a little too much. *I'm sure listening to me snore all night from the other room didn't get me on her good side, either.* As she rubbed my nose in my deplorable behavior, she exclaimed, "Do you think you are camping?!" I begged her forgiveness and explained that I had every intention of replacing everything I smoked and drank. She was kind enough to give me the benefit of the doubt and a second chance.

After a disastrous and late start to the day and several apologies later, we rebounded, and she gave me a tour of the city. Instead of being completely immersed in Rome's beauty and history, I was distracted by my conflicting feelings of needing a drink and trying to play it cool since I had already fucked up. I had misjudged the party person I thought I was coming to visit. Drinking is a part of the culture there, but not the irresponsible, binge drink-until-you're-in-jail type of drinking. Sometimes I'd forget the way my friends and I drank would hospitalize most other people. Throughout the day, I would gently steer us towards activities that allowed me to get a drink. "So that's the Colosseum, huh? Cool. Does it have a bar?"

Later that night, we met with a couple of her friends to get something to eat. I suddenly had a wave of anxiety wash over me, almost to the point of a panic attack. I knew it was from a lack of alcohol in my system. When everybody was seated, I excused myself, returned to the order counter, which I thought was out of sight from where we were sitting, and bought two beers. I pounded both in under a couple of minutes. I then ordered two more to bring back with me. One of her friends saw this, and when I got back to the table, she looked at me and said,

"Ahhh, drinker, huh?"

"Yeah, I'm just trying to get a good balance," I said, embarrassed that I got caught displaying a total lack of self-control. The rest of the night is a little blurry, but I don't recall anything catastrophic happening.

The next day, I again woke up to her knocking on the door, making me aware of how late it was. When I came out, three of her friends were there, and everybody was kind of quiet and somber. I immediately knew something was off. I knew they were about to stage an intervention. We had some food and uncomfortable small talk at the table, and then it happened. She said she was uncomfortable with my drinking and wanted me to leave. Her friends were there in case I reacted badly to the news. She was still kind and said she'd help me find a place to stay and take me to the airport when needed. All I could do was apologize and pack up my shit. I knew there was no point in trying to plead my case and ask for forgiveness. I fucked up, and this was the consequence.

I asked her to find me somewhere cheap to stay because I had little money. She found a hostel and took me there to ensure everything was okay. On the train ride, I fought back tears in disbelief at what was happening. Sensing how distraught I was, one of her friends asked me if I wanted an ice cream when we got off the train. It made me feel like a kid having a bad day and having an adult say to me, "You okay, kiddo? Ya wanna ice cream?" I know she meant well, but it slightly twisted the knife in my already fragile self-esteem.

I knew we were in a bad part of town the second we got off the train. If there's one thing I've learned over the years, it's how to recognize the distinct look and vibe of a sketchy neighborhood. Her friend told me to be mindful of my wallet and backpack because there were marauding, pickpocketing "gypsies" everywhere. When we got to the hostel, we all had a bad feeling. Rundown and shady would be a complimentary description. My friend started to speak to the unkempt, surly man at the front desk. Even though they spoke Italian, and I had no idea what they were saying, I knew it didn't sound pleasant. After whatever they spoke, the clerk took us down a hall and knocked on one of the doors. A fat man wearing nothing but a towel around his waist with a cigarette dangling from his mouth opened the door, looked at us, said nothing, and then disappeared back into the smokey, dim cavern. It was a small, dark, dingy space with three beds inside. Another shirtless man occupied one of the other cots in the room.

For a second, I thought it was some sort of poetic punishment I had earned. I looked at my friend and begged her to find me something else; there was no way I was staying in that strange, dark pit in the slums of Rome. We eventually found a hotel in a less dangerous part of town where I wouldn't have to share a room with two shirtless strangers. Still emotional and overwhelmed, I said a teary goodbye to her and apologized as sincerely as I could. I didn't feel like I did anything that egregious to warrant exile, but I wasn't going to argue. I had mangled an expectation we both fantasized about when we were on different sides of the world. As Thanos said: "Reality is often disappointing."

I walked around the ancient streets alone and drank for the next few days, wondering how I fucked this up. It was almost humorous at one point when I was walking down a cobblestone street with my head hung low, passing under a bridge where a lone accordion player was filling the air with his woeful tune. Federico Fellini could not have written a more appropriate scene. On the third day of my sad, solo adventure, my friend who kicked me out of her home asked if I wanted to hang out again; she felt bad about the situation and agreed to give me another chance. Overcome with gratitude, I made a vehement effort to keep my drinking to a minimum. When I returned to her apartment, her dog was not as forgiving and peed on my hat—I didn't realize this until I was back on the plane and wondered why I smelled like Chihuahua urine.

On the flight back, I got stuck in Istanbul for over a day due to a flight delay. I had to get a visa to go into town and stay the night, and it was late when the cab driver dropped me off in a sketchy part of town. When I checked in, all I cared about was where I could get a drink. When I asked the hotel clerk where a bar or kiosk that sold beers was, he looked at me and said, "I wouldn't wander around here if I were you," indicating I'd be in danger because of how I looked; I wasn't going to let that stop me. After about five minutes of walking around and getting the side eye from some scary characters, I found a little store that sold me some beers. I quickly went back to the hotel room and locked the door. After the way the trip had been going, I was in no mood for any more bullshit.

During these years, I took whatever work I could find. I finally landed a "real" job as a sales rep at a national solar company. It was a soul-crushing corporate environment. In my twenties, I had gotten my hands tattooed for the sole purpose of not winding up in an office as a corporate stiff. The societal opinion of tattoos that once rendered me unemployable has softened over the years, but they used to call hand and neck tattoos "Job Stoppers."

I interviewed slightly buzzed, and was viciously hungover on my first day of employment; that should paint the picture of my work experience for the next couple of years. I was morbidly hungover every Monday morning from drinking until blackout every weekend. It was crippling and excruciating. I had to drink a beer on those mornings before work to stop the shakes and the sweats; it numbed me up just enough to ward off a panic attack. When I'd punch in for work, I would wait until nobody was around me at the time clock because I was afraid someone would notice how badly my hands were shaking.

I started having a drink with my lunch to stave off withdrawal. This was new territory for me—my drinking had become so advanced that it required maintenance. To feel like a functional adult, I had to have a small dose of alcohol. I wasn't drinking to get hammered or for fun, I was drinking because my body physically needed it. I had turned a corner, descending a path with precarious footing.

I was able to maintain a relatively functional work-life despite my problems. I was seldom late or called out because I was hungover—I still had some integrity and lines I wouldn't cross. I even worked myself up the ladder a bit. I'll never forget a meeting I had with the owner of this multi-million-dollar solar company and another manager, discussing a new department they were developing; they wanted me to supervise it. I was in a debilitating hangover daze, looking at my tattooed hands, wondering how the fuck I had arrived at this moment. Not really comprehending what they were saying, I kept my composure, nodded frequently, and said, "Sounds good."

Even with the fancy new title and some slick designer blazers I had bought for the new position, I was still miserable and the job made me feel morally bankrupt. I felt like I sold out. I wasn't even making that much money to justify the dignity I was losing for myself, but I made enough to pay my bills, rent, and drink. Why look beyond that, right? To manage my misery from any source, I drank. Any aspirations to pull myself out of this predicament were dulled by drinking. It put me in a tiny box and made me believe that everything outside of it was unobtainable and that I was unqualified for a better life. I was being gaslit by alcohol. It made me feel like I couldn't do any better; like there was no use even trying. It's a vicious cycle, working for the weekend.

The last girl I dated before I quit drinking was different; she had a handle on her liquor intake. She never partied hard, or even pretended that she did. One drink was all she'd have most times we hung out. Sometimes she'd have two or three, but those occasions were rare. It was refreshing to be around someone so unlike myself. The rock-n-roll lifestyle wasn't something she was at all interested in. She was beautiful inside and out. She had an authentic, quirky charm that endeared me to her. Her voice and laughter filled a room with warmth and spirit. I could listen to her talk for hours.

In the beginning, I made a little effort to try and cut back on my drinking when I was around her. That didn't last very long. I would pound a few beers before hanging out or try to sneak in sips of something when she wasn't looking. I always tried to keep as much composure as I could. Sometimes, I would think of sentences I wanted to say for several minutes before I attempted to huck them out of my mouth, trying to outsmart my slurring tongue. Maybe she didn't notice or just ignored it. Of course, other embarrassing problems would throw wrenches into the gears now and again, like being unable to *get it up* in the boudoir or having digestive issues because of my alcohol intake.

This was another new experience for me; I never had to hide drinking before. The shame of what I was doing finally soaked into my thick head. *What the fuck am I actually doing?!* It wasn't the first time I realized how bad my problem had become, but it was the first time I cared. I wanted to be in control! I finally saw through the illusion of my devil-may-care, reckless, rockstar persona I sold myself to justify my behavior. I didn't like this feeling, nor was it romantic or cool or whatever bullshit I told myself. It was an uncontrollable compulsion.

I was growing more self-conscious when we were together. I was in love and sincerely respected her; I wanted to stop drinking, but I couldn't. Our connection was crumbling. I still kept up my pace and she soon saw the loveable lush had a legitimate problem. The relationship ended when we planned a getaway to her hometown to hang out with her family. Shortly before the trip, she concluded that it wasn't a good idea anymore and that we should break up. She said she didn't believe I could stop drinking and that she needed to move on. I wasn't shocked by this declaration. How could I have been? I knew the ice I was skating on was losing the strength to bear the weight of my bullshit.

I remember that call vividly. "I fucking hate this! I don't want to be like this anymore!" I whimpered through my sobs. I felt defeated and pathetic as I held my phone with a delirium-trembling hand. It brought back all the memories of guilt and shame I felt with my past failed relationship; I didn't want to repeat the same mistakes, but here I was again, knowing I had ruined everything. All our trips and outings together, our sex life, and the relationship's overall health were beaten to death by my inability to deal with the real problem: me.

I was sick of feeling like I wasn't good enough for anyone and self-sabotaging everything in my life. I was tired of making apologies for my behavior like it was a belligerent child I had no control over. I didn't want to hurt one more person I was in love with and that loved me back because I couldn't wrap my head around just not putting anything with alcohol into my stupid mouth.

I had no plan or idea what I would do next, but I did have a scalding wad of anger burning in me and a furious determination to change who I was.

Don't hold on

It's getting hard
To cover up these scars
The skies are gray
And they seem to be every day
I'm so sick of the rain
I know every drop by name
But I'll force a smile
Yeah, they've been forced for a while

Don't hold on to me

It's hard waking up
When all you do ain't enough
I drank myself to the end
Of this rope where I now spin
It's so hard moving on
When all your dreams are gone

Don't hold on to me

Misery is my friend
And she will be to my end
There's nothing left to know
So please just let me go

Don't hold on to me

6

The Last Drink

"Death is nothing, but to live defeated and inglorious is to die daily"

~ Napolean Bonaparte

There is nothing special about the last time I was drunk. It was another ordinary weekend where I drank to blackout both Friday and Saturday. Sunday was, of course, "Sunday Funday," so I would start early and end early to be able to wake up for work the next day. I was a responsible degenerate, after all.

I was my usual inebriated self on Sunday, June 23, 2019, around 6:00 p.m. I decided to get two last tall cans of beer for the night. I was already very drunk at this juncture. For some reason, I put on my pants without a belt and slid on an oversized pair of flip-flops. They were so big that I had to curl my toes as I walked to keep them from falling off. So there I was, holding up my pants so they didn't fall to my ankles as I hobbled down the street, painfully clutching the ridiculous clown thongs between my toes. The resident homeless fellow I befriended over the years, Tony, was in his tent by the corner store, asking for his toll of whatever change you could spare to pass on his sidewalk. He chuckled at me and said, "Man, you're looking roasty toasty." That was the appraisal of my demeanor by the neighborhood drunk. *Or maybe I was seeing the ghost of Christmas Future the whole time, giving me a sneak preview of my life if I keep stumbling down this path. At any rate, it's not a positive endorsement.*

I bought my tall cans and headed back home. I was drinking with one hand; with the other, I held the second can and my pants up with a contorted claw-like grip, all while walking with the stupid flip-flops. I was a sight to behold, stumbling like a toddler who was blindfolded and spun around before being pushed toward a piñata and *WHACK*! I had hit my foot on a pushed-up piece of sidewalk. I face-planted hard! The 24 oz can of Natural Light that I was drinking smacked the sidewalk and started to fizz up and spray everywhere. A guy on a balcony across the street saw the whole thing. "Dude…are you okay?" I picked up what was left of my beer and dignity and sat on a little wall lining the sidewalk.

"Yeah, I'm okay," I whimpered. I put a hole in my pants to show off a bloodied-up scraped knee. I scratched up my hand and my face to match. I sat there in total mental and physical defeat. *How the fuck did I arrive at such a destitute existence?* At that moment, I literally and figuratively hit rock bottom.

I made it home and finished most of the beer I had risked my body and soul for, saving myself half a can of breakfast beer for the Monday morning sweats and shakes. I passed out drunk on my couch and woke up in the middle of the night to put myself to bed—my standard weekend ritual. The next day, the pain was exponentially worse; I felt like I had gone ten rounds with Mike Tyson. It wasn't unusual to feel this shitty, but my tolerance for accepting it was gone. I was fed the fuck up!

On Monday, June 24, I drank my morning coffee and a couple of gulps of semi-flat beer, hopped on my eighteen-speed, and pedaled off to work. I was forty years old, bicycling under the unrelenting heat of the June sun because I didn't own, nor could legally drive a car. All to go to a dead-end job I hated, to make just enough money to afford booze and rent. There wasn't a shred of hope in any direction as far as the eye could see. The sad, painful, and pathetic reality of my life at that moment spun around in my head like the wheels on my bike.

I pretended to be productive in that life-sucking office, but every time I got up to walk, I was reminded of my weakness of body and mind. My choices were defeating me. I was trying to hold on to some sort of rockstar lifestyle that wasn't fulfilling anymore, clutching desperately to the last semblance of my youth. I was afraid to change, to grow up and grow old. This wasn't the way things were supposed to go.

I had nine hours to stew in my thoughts as I watched the time clock tick away my life. I didn't have any plans to stop drinking before this. Just two weeks prior, I was in San Francisco for a gig, where I snorted mystery drugs someone found in an ally in the Tenderloin district. I was also having key bumps of cocaine brought right up to my nostrils at the after-show party. If someone had told me that night that I'd be taking my last drink two weeks from then, I would have snickered, said, "Unlikely," and then asked them to share their drugs with me.

I had never wholeheartedly tried to stop drinking before, but I concluded I would get my usual half pint of vodka on the way home from work, and that would be my last for thirty days... The only time I had been sober for more than a couple of days in the last twenty-one years was when I was in jail. I told only one person what I was attempting to do, and she didn't believe I could do it. I wouldn't have been very optimistic either from her vantage point, but maybe my competitive spirit took that as a challenge.

Either way, I had something to prove now to myself.

When I got home from work, I unknowingly drank my last sip of alcohol. The person I used to be died in his sleep that night. Whatever past I was clinging to, whatever version of me I was so afraid to lose, I decided he wasn't going to wake up again. He would stay in a dream, evaporating on the wisp of a memory, fading like smoke into the ether.

Wretched Places

My bags are packed, it's time to go
I hope never to return
This wretched place is all I know
But it's time to watch it burn

With bitter sentiment farewell
Adorned with scars from this abuse
Faded fractured memories
Beautiful things turned tragedies
I have none to blame and no excuse

I'm free
The weight is gone
I'm moving on
I've been drowning far too long

I'm free
I'm on my way
To better days
I don't want to live this way

My bags are packed, it's time to go

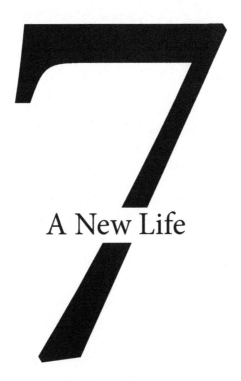

7

A New Life

"If you are not in the process of becoming the person you want to be, you are automatically engaged in becoming the person you don't want to be."

~ DALE CARNEGIE

Why should I stop drinking? Am I ready to stop drinking? Do I need to stop? These are the questions that nobody can answer for you. Everybody will have unique circumstances, experiences, and biological makeup that dictate their actions and motivations. Some people might be more advanced in their dependency and require professional help. Others could have one or two drinks total during the week and not need to change anything. Then there is someone like me who drank heavily but could function at a mediocre level. Some would say I'm an alcoholic, and others would not. How anyone wants to define and label me is up to them; I don't really care. All I know is that I was exhausted, ashamed, disappointed, and angry at myself. I needed a better way to live or, at the very least, a better way to die. The thought of being found dead with a bottle in my hand became increasingly less attractive. The drunk, or overdosed pseudo rockstar found blue on a bathroom floor didn't carry the same romantic whimsy as it did in my twenties and thirties.

My tumble on the sidewalk was the catalyst I didn't know I needed to make a change. Sometimes, it takes a slap in your dumb face to realize what you're doing and how dire your situation is. You could be saying to yourself, "It seems to me, you were slapped several times in your stupid face," and you'd be right. My fear of letting it go was too intense. A Sequoia needs several hefty whacks with an axe before it comes down. Looking back, I'm almost glad I partied as hard as I did. If I were drinking one or two notches less, I don't think I would have been able to see the subtle insidiousness that alcohol kept me sedated with. I'd probably still be working for the weekend, not striving for anything better. I had finally broken the spell. I chose the red pill.

On Tuesday, June 25, I still had a mild hangover from the weekend and the cocktail I had the night prior, but I had a new sense of determination and purpose. I would not let myself drink that day—just twenty-four small steps toward my goal. I hobbled out of bed and peddled, still in pain, to work. I would forgo alcoholic beverages in the morning and lunch. When the clock hit 5:00 p.m., it was showtime. Let's put my newfound resolve to the test!

On my way home I'd always get something to sip on. The thirsty defense lawyer in my head came to persuade and bargain with me to pick up a cold one. "Who do you think you're fooling? There's no way you're gonna stop completely, so why try at all? One drink isn't going to kill you!" It's a damn fine argument, but all I had to do was make it until the morning. *NOT TODAY!* is what I told that fiending bastard voice in my head. Tomorrow doesn't exist, and yesterday is only a memory. All I needed to do was concentrate on the present. If my compulsion to drink became unbearably persistent, I would compartmentalize every second.

The urge dissipated reasonably fast if I could resist its initial, push. "Maybe tomorrow, but not today" became my mantra for several months.

My work week was relatively easy to get through. The weekend would be my first real test of discipline. Usually, the only thing I looked forward to all week was getting hammered, starting promptly at lunch on Friday and then carrying on until Sunday evening. *What the fuck am I going to do now?!* I didn't realize how much time I had wasted on alcohol, or recovering from it, after drinking was no longer part of my routine. The first weekend felt like a month. I didn't have a plan or know what to do. It was the true beginning of my journey.

On Saturday morning, I made sure to wake up early and exercise. In my adult life, I can't recall ever getting up before 7:00 a.m., fully refreshed, and ready to take on the day. I was either still up partying at that hour or passed the fuck out. Waking up feeling 100% quickly became my new drug of choice. I no longer had to change my schedule to prioritize drinking, being hungover, or worse, a complete coke night derailment of my next two days. Early morning activities were now available to me. I felt like Jack Skellington discovering Christmas Town for the first time. "What's this, what's this?!"

Waking up early is a common thread in almost all personal development books. Who was I to doubt the wisdom of these sacred texts? Waking up at 5:00 a.m. became my new norm. Not only did I feel like I was getting a head start on the rest of the world, but in the evening, I would be so tired from a productive, fulfilling day that around 8:00 or 9:00, there was no time to want a drink. It is something I practice to this day.

I kept myself extremely busy that first weekend. I didn't want the Devil to catch my hands idling. I rediscovered hobbies I had shelved over the years. I blew the dust off my guitar and books. I played video games. I ramped up exercising in all forms, running, cycling, and weights. Admittedly, at first, I chased the easy type of dopamine by eating shitty food and watching too much porn, but I would soon refine my activities to more noble pursuits. Anything to keep my mind from wanting a drink in those first couple of months was imperative.

The first Monday back to work after being dead sober for a week felt strikingly different. I had energy. I had a bounce in my step. Sure, I was still aware it was a demoralizing dead-end job, but today, I had hope! It no longer felt like I was stuck in this job. My mentality switched from "feeling lucky to be there" to "they're lucky I'm here!" I had confidence, focus, and a vastly more optimistic understanding of my potential. It was a night and day difference.

The first non-hungover week flew by fast. Every day after work, I exercised or kept myself busy until I had exhausted all my energy. Keeping my mind off drinking was paramount. I didn't have a group, sponsor, or anybody to confide in if I felt triggered, so I ensured there was no time *to* get triggered. It was my hill to climb and mine alone. And that hill was about to get steeper because the Fourth of July long holiday weekend awaited me. How could I adequately pay my respect to the good ole U.S. of A. without washing down half a dozen hot hogs with a couple of cases of domestic light beer?

As with most anxieties and fears, the gargantuan monster I created in my head about the long weekend was nothing more than a whiney, spoiled child crying for candy at a checkout line. I audibly told myself, "Dude, NO! You don't need it!" Seeing and talking to myself as a friend, child, or pet was remarkably helpful. I wouldn't let a friend drink if they were trying to stop. I wouldn't let my pet eat poison, so why shouldn't I have the same level of compassion and well-being for myself? My inner dialogue became increasingly more positive and helpful. It was a direct result of steeping myself into the self-help genre. No matter how ridiculous or corny a lot of it can be, with enough persistence, it starts to seep into your subconscious.

I would start my day with ten minutes of "I AM" affirmations, then read various self-improvement books on my breaks, and then fall asleep to more positive affirmations. It was monotonous, and sometimes, the sugar-coated positivity made me want to vomit, but I stuck with it every day for a few months. I also became vigilantly guarded about all the media I consumed. I stopped watching/reading the news and unfollowed any page or person that made me angry, depressed, or envious. I removed anything attached to negative feelings from my intake.

Independence Day came and went without any slip-ups or uncontrollable urges. I had made it two weeks without a drip of alcohol. That was much farther than I thought I was going to get. I had never felt better in my life! The emotional raging tides that usually wreaked chaos in my head were now gentle, manageable waves. I was sleeping better. My skin looked better. Everything was just plain fucking better!

Having this newfound sense of well-being and accomplishment, I decided to clean up all the loose ends I had neglected over the years. My first priority was my driver's license. I had been driving without one for over ten years. I never bothered to check on its status because I figured the penalties the court had served were too severe for my willingness to comply. But I finally relented and called the DMV, and surprisingly, all I had to do was finish the eighteen-month second-offender class. I completed it the first time, but I didn't pay the entire fee, so they didn't report my completion to the DMV, so I had to do it all over again. I wasn't thrilled about that news, but on the unbelievably bright side, I'd be given a restricted license the second I enrolled in the class. *Fuck yeah!* I signed up the next day, and *POOF!* My driving was legit for the first time in over a decade.

With my license reinstated and a couple of weeks off the sauce, I rewarded myself with a gift and a challenge. I wanted to do something I always dreamed of doing, but I was somehow smart enough to know I'd die or be severely hurt if I attempted it while drinking. Something my pops and my pop's pop had done their whole lives. I bought a motorcycle!

Riding cemented my 180-degree lifestyle turnabout. It was the missing piece of my puzzle I was having difficulty finding. It took up my time, energy, and focus. At first, I had trouble learning to ride the 700-pound V-twin monster and almost gave up, but I committed and dug deep. Going on a freeway the first time almost gave me a heart attack. I got off at the very next exit. I had to catch my breath and check my underpants. Learning how to do U-turns and traversing winding mountain roads became my new drug. It turned into one of my most rewarding accomplishments. It served as a springboard to pursue anything I put my mind to. I also promised myself that if I fucked up and started to drink again, I would have to sell the bike. There's no way I'd let myself near a motorcycle, buzzed, drunk, or hungover.

At this point, just a few weeks from my last drink, I knew I wasn't returning to the miserable swamp I had crawled out of.

There was no way I could face myself if I had even a sip of alcohol. I accomplished quite a bit in a very short time frame and aspired to do much more. I had created reasons never to go back to the drink. It was the first time I experienced a positive snowball effect. I was always accustomed to the variety that started with mild irritation and then quickly turned into a "What the fuck just happened?!" dumpster fire.

I was starting to feel comfortable with myself around the three-month mark. I didn't have a problem hanging around people that drank. I wasn't triggered by going to my usual restaurants or walking by my corner liquor store. I only thought about the hangovers, the belligerence, and the severely out-of-whack emotional balance. I made it a point to only focus on the negatives when the thought of drinking popped into my head. That wasn't hard to do. Finding a positive reason to drink would prove to be much more difficult. The cost of a "fun night out" is much more than just the drinks.

I never had the *I'll just cut back*, or *I'll only have one, or two drinks,* idea. I wanted all the drinks or none of them. One drink only made me lethargic and seemed like a waste of money and calories. I drank to get fucked up. There was no other point as far as I was concerned. I also never heard or read one story or biography from anybody—rock stars, actors, whatever—that ended well when they decided to have "just a couple drinks" after being sober for a while. They all end in regret. Learning from other people's mistakes is an excellent way to avoid pitfalls.

It was time to give myself a test with my new hobby and the confidence I had cultivated. I decided to ride my motorcycle from LA to Vegas by myself. I only had three months of riding experience and was still afraid to turn left at intersections, but I wasn't going to let that stop me. Who needs to turn left, anyway? I also wasn't sure if I could resist all the seductive debauchery that Las Vegas has to offer. But the open road was singing me songs of wind in my face and bugs in my teeth! I love a good challenge, and this seemed like a worthy opponent. I figured if I made it to Vegas alive, I couldn't drink because I wouldn't let myself get on the bike if I did. That makes sense, right?

Once in Vegas, I felt an uncomfortable compulsion at first. When I got to my hotel, it was like walking into an ex-girlfriend's home. All the sights, sounds, and smells had shaken the coffins—rousing the drunken ghosts I had buried. Was it a mistake to come here? I instantly wanted to drink all the drinks and smoke a pack of cigarettes; and do I still have the number of any drug dealers here? I may have overestimated my temperance. I checked in, went straight to my room, and took a shower. It was time to regroup.

The first urge I hurdled was the want for a smoke. Being in a casino and breathing the nicotine-heavy air made me never want a cigarette again. Even when I was a professional smoker, being in that environment wasn't enjoyable. Seeing a sun-dried old man smoking in broad daylight in the suffocating heat of the Nevada desert should be enough for anyone to give up the habit. You could not have paid me enough to light up a cigarette. Plus, smoking (and drugs) are the dickhead friends of booze. If alcohol isn't at the party, then neither are his rotten buddies.

I made it down to the pool to relax and reflect on how unlikely my situation was. *Am I really in Vegas, not drinking? Did I ride a fucking motorcycle here?! Who the fuck am I?* And then I saw the physical embodiment of my disdain for alcohol. A group of college kids, piss drunk, blew in like an obnoxious tornado. It was the middle of the afternoon, and they were beyond hammered. No judgment, of course, because that would've been me just three and a half months prior. A feeling of relief washed over me. I was so profoundly grateful not to be feeling or acting like that. It was like watching an old cringy video of a version of me that I felt completely removed from. In a couple of hours, they'd soon be passed out or riding on the back of narcotics to carry them through the night. I, on the other hand, felt well-rested, sharp, and had a much deeper feeling of happiness. It's the kind of well-being you can't pour into a yard-long, fluorescent green plastic cup or snort through a straw.

I retired early that evening. Riding a motorcycle over 300 miles took a lot out of me. The following day, I awoke to a strange but fantastic feeling, one I'd never experienced before. It was as if the sun and all the animals were singing a beautiful tune, tickling my eardrums, and gently lifting me out of my slumber. I felt like a Disney princess! It was 6:00 a.m., but I wasn't still up from the night before. I had slept eight hours in Las Vegas, of all places! I skipped down to the casino and got a coffee and a pastry. Seeing all the zombies still trying to keep the party going at that hour sparked joy in my heart. It felt like looking through an old picture album where I could smile and have a nostalgic fondness for the past, but I was so happy to be where I was now–seeing with wiser eyes. Pro tip: If you ever want an entire gym to yourself, go to one at a Vegas hotel at 7:00 a.m.

Five months after my last drink, I got my first car in over ten years. My parents had gifted me a little Toyota that was smashed because they got T-boned in an intersection. It was ugly, and I couldn't open the passenger door, but it was a functioning car. I called it "Crunch Wrap." I now had two options of transportation. It was more positive momentum propelling me forward. It seemed like everything changed once I started seeing the world working with me instead of against me. With my new forms of mobility, my job opportunities opened up because I no longer had to choose bus or bicycle-friendly employment locations. It was time to leave the corporate office environment, which I despised.

My plans for a career change were suddenly halted due to an end-of-days scenario no one had seen coming: COVID-19. For the next year, I'd be working from home. I cannot imagine how much I would've drank if that had happened nine months prior. It seemed like the entire world escalated its drinking, and I would have been no exception. I was already drinking at work when I had to go into an office, but "working" in the privacy of my own home? I would have pickled myself into liver failure. The lockdown only strengthened my resolve. I had more time to read, watch, and learn about personal development and psychology to further shape myself into the person I wanted to be and knew I could become.

When Covid finally cooled down, and things started to open back up, new employment opportunities were scarce. I felt trapped and scared to leave the job that I hated. All the usual thoughts born from fear went through my head: *But what if this happens? I'll be screwed if this happens!*

Sometimes, your thoughts are not your friend, nor do they give you good advice. Much like, *C'mon, just one drink. No one will know,* or *You're too tired to exercise. Let's get a pizza and watch a movie,* or *Why do you think anybody wants to listen to you? You're a nobody.* When your thoughts are trying to steer you back into a comfort zone, or they are negative self-talk, you have to tell yourself to shut the fuck up. Battling addictions, resisting laziness, and self-deprecation is a head game that, unfortunately, will never end. The good news is you will get exponentially better at it as time passes.

While wrestling with fear of the unknown and working a job I hated, the universe intervened and gave me a sign.

One evening, on my way home from work, a lady driving toward me thought she had a protected left-turn green arrow, which she did not, and turned right in front of me. It happened so fast I didn't even have time to brake. If I were on my bike, I probably would have died on the spot. My beautiful, already partially totaled Yaris was now completely totaled. Just when everything seemed to be going my way, *BAM!* Another airbag to my face. I suffered a concussion, some bruises, and a torn muscle in my shoulder. The following days after the accident, I kept on replaying it in my head. Did I look at my phone? Did I sneeze or yawn? Was I lost in thought and not paying attention or speeding? The answer was a resounding *NO.* Nothing I could have done differently would've prevented it from happening.

It was the epiphany I needed. It suddenly dawned on me that no matter what I did, no matter how safe and cautious I tried to be, everything, including my life, could be taken in a heartbeat.

So, what the fuck am I afraid of? What's holding me back from going after exactly what I want? If I had died on the street in North Hollywood that night, it damn well better have been on my pursuit of something great rather than in fear of hypothetical *what-ifs.* It was such an astonishing change in my perspective that I felt stupid for not seeing it before. All of us die and will be forgotten soon after. *Am I going to be proud of myself and feel like I did my best before I take my last breath, or will I be ashamed of all the things I didn't accomplish or even try because I was afraid?* I knew I wouldn't have been proud of myself that night or any of the other countless times I could've perished in the previous twenty years.

"It comes down to a simple choice, really: Get busy living, or get busy dying."

Over the next two years, I remodeled my whole life. I could no longer tolerate "just getting by." I'm embarrassed to say that for a moment, when I first stopped drinking, I began to conform to societal standards by accepting a "normal" life, and it made me miserable. I had turned my back on my passions and proclivities. I was neglecting the adventurous spirit that I've always had. Before, I was feeding that side of me by drinking and doing stupid shit, but when I left the party life I still craved excitement and exploration, but I hadn't learned where and how to channel that energy. The motorcycle was my first step, but I needed something more.

I recognized that an office job was my personal hell. If I couldn't fully support myself with music or something creative, I at least had to do something I enjoyed. I have always loved driving, touring, and road trips, so I called the DMV to see if I was eligible for a commercial driver's license. Given my driving history, I wasn't optimistic about my chance, but as it turned out, all my adverse driving history had expired. Upon learning that, I enrolled myself in trucking school the next day. Four months later, I was a fully endorsed, TSA-cleared truck driver. I immediately quit my corporate gig without even having a job lined up yet.

How's that for a plot twist? The guy with four DUIs, who was often too drunk to walk down a sidewalk, could now drive an 80,000-pound, twenty-two-wheeled truck full of explosives into an airport—*legally*! If driving through the Colorado Rockies in a semi-truck at night, in the snow with an overweight fifty-three-foot container, isn't an adventure, I don't know what is. It made me realize what an office job could never offer me: life-jeopardizing peril!

The next thing I had to do was change my living situation. As I mentioned, I had been in the same one-bedroom apartment for seventeen years. It was in a rent-controlled building, and the owner never raised the rent. The negative side of cheap housing was it allowed me to be a slacker and not aim higher than "good enough." The building was in bad shape, and overcrowded. It was always loud and chaotic. I felt trapped because I knew my living expenses would more than double if I left, which made me reluctant to look for work that was too far away. It also discouraged me from moving somewhere else with a partner if I wanted to. It became limiting and, in some ways, kept me tied to my past.

I eventually found a driving job I liked by the beach, but the commute back and forth was killing me. Coming home sometimes took two hours. As an LA native, living by the ocean had always been a life goal of mine, but it seemed out of reach. And now, here I was, working in the port of LA, which I loved, yet considering quitting my job to find one closer to my shithole apartment. After a few months of thinking about my situation, the lesson of "*Memento Mori*" (remember you will die) from the car accident pointed me in the right direction. I gave my landlord my thirty-day notice and moved to the beach. There was no way I was going to let myself die in the valley. *Fuck that!*

When I put the last box in the U-Haul and closed apartment door number 19 for the last time, I was overcome with emotion. It was the last part of my old life I let go of. I had made it out of a place I thought for sure I was going to die in, both literally and figuratively. Without any help from a program, therapy, or rehab, I clawed my way out of a hole that I thought had no end. In three years, my life was unrecognizable from the chaotic mess it used to be. My anger toward myself became fuel to propel me to a better life. By sheer will, determination, and discipline, I focused on becoming the person I was supposed to be. I was relentless in educating myself. I was critically introspective and focused on where I needed to improve. Most importantly of all, I believed I could do it. I was not broken or helpless.

I knew my transformation was well within my capabilities if I put every ounce of energy toward it. I also remained humble enough to know when to ask for help from a friend. I can honestly tell you that if I happen to die today, I will do so with a smile because I know I'm on the right path, trying my best and living as authentically as I possibly can. That's all anyone can do.

The further I got away from drinking, the less I even thought about it. I couldn't imagine going back. The new life I had created had no time for that nonsense. I started to live with a purpose. The sense of accomplishment I got from physically and mentally challenging myself became my new source of dopamine. I soon noticed that my addiction was more of a conceptual problem than anything else. Viewing myself as confident, disciplined, and capable removed all the self-imposed limitations I had attached myself to. I became deliberate with where I aimed my attention–changing my confirmation bias toward the positive instead of the negative. It's just as easy to look for the good in everything–so why look for the bad? I rebuilt my character from the ground up with a much better foundation and blueprint.

I learned to isolate the self-demoralizing internal monologue and flip it into motivation. I got competitive against the part of me that didn't want to leave its comfort zone. I learned that I am not my thoughts–they only appear in consciousness and disappear as soon as they arise, like waves in an ocean. Now, when one pops into my head, I grab hold of it to determine if it's trying to work for or against me. Filling my head with better content fundamentally changed the quality of my thinking. I carefully chose what I watched, listened to, and read, as well as the conversations I would have and the company I kept.

All the relationships I was worried about either changing or dissolving were no concern. The people who stuck around are the ones who genuinely love me. If the friends you have are only enjoyable when you or they are drunk, they are not your real friends. The dynamic with my family changed a bit, but it's been a positive metamorphosis. Most people I've mentioned in these stories are still a part of my life. They have seen the absolute worst of me and still stuck around. That's fucking love!

Romantic relationships changed most in the best possible

ways. I became more authentic and allowed myself to be vulnerable. I also got a much better sense of what the person I was with was actually like because I could remember our conversations. Values change along with wants and needs when you elevate the standard for yourself and your partner. The off-the-rails screaming fights don't happen. The feeling of "this thing will explode at any moment" doesn't exist. All the chaos that corroded my past relationships was caused by drinking. Sex gets much better, too. Being in tune with your partner and yourself is a much more satisfying experience. I used to think the uninhibited drunk and drug-influenced frenzies were the best. In contrast to those moments, having sex dead sober seemed dull. But after getting comfortable with myself, all the things I was too afraid or embarrassed to do weren't so scary anymore. Being brave and bold in the bedroom started to come naturally. Authentic intimacy with someone without drinking is deeply satisfying. Not to mention, the shame and disappointment of a nonworking appendage isn't an issue anymore.

The outgoing person I was only when I drank was just beneath the surface the whole time. All I needed was a little effort and self-assurance. Confidence was a happy byproduct of accomplishment when I started being more productive. Creating and conquering goals is time-consuming and gave me a sustainable, guilt-free dopamine drip. Keeping busy, learning, reading, watching, and aiming higher are some of the traits I've embedded into the fibers of my being. Staying true to myself and continually nurturing my unique characteristics is a priority. Associating alcohol with all the negative shit instead of the "*fun night out*" or "*I need this to relax*" was also important. I can no longer see any redeeming qualities in drinking.

The mental health issues that I've dealt with my whole adult life virtually disappeared with the absence of alcohol. The thought of harming myself no longer exists. The worry and dread that used to haunt my thoughts at night no longer keep me from sleep. The all-consuming hopelessness and despair that followed me like a shadow has ceased to torment me. My mood and temperament have been ingrained with genuine positivity. Of course, I still have bad days and moments of weakness, but the intensity of toxic thoughts and emotions has since been domesticated into docile, manageable critters.

Who knows, maybe if I reach my seventies or eighties, I'll jump head-first off this teetotaler wagon I'm on, becoming that drunk, smoking-in-the-heat old man you'll wince at on Freemont Street in Vegas. But for now, I have shit to do. I'm not willing to give up my time, money, and physical/mental health for the empty promises, lies, and pain that alcohol comes with. When I tripped on the sidewalk years ago, that was the universe telling me *Hey stupid, it's last call*. I'm forever grateful that I finally listened.

Exit Strategy

"Before you heal someone, ask him if he's willing to give up the things that make him sick."

~ HIPPOCRATES

I thank you from the bottom of my heart if you're still reading this. By now, you know I have some experience with drinking, drugs, and all the fun stuff that comes with it. My goal for this book is to offer hope and a new perspective for anyone wanting to stop drinking. When I started looking into quitting, every avenue I turned down said I was a powerless alcoholic and needed a 12-step program or rehab. There wasn't a sliding scale regarding the nuance and intensity of my habit. The standardized diagnosis also didn't recognize my determination, will, and discipline as being legitimate enough to beat my "disease." So, I decided to do my own research and blaze a new trail. Again, this is not professional advice. I'm not an addiction counselor or doctor, nor do I have any type of credential. What I do have is over twenty years of experience with drinking and drug use and empirical evidence of how I was able to overcome my problems on my own.

What worked for me may not work for you. If your program—AA, rehab, or whatever it may be—is helping you, then by all means, continue to engage with it. You can use this information in conjunction with whatever you're already involved with. We have a common enemy, and that enemy is alcohol! I had a hard time finding materials and resources that resonated with me and, thus, inspired me to put this into the universe. If my words are helpful in any way, small or large, I'm grateful to you and wish you the very best on your voyage to a better life.

My first pearl of wisdom is: just stop drinking, goddamn it! It's that simple. If you've had your fun, but it's become burdensome, I urge you to hang it up. My experiences over the years have been terrifying, beautiful, tragic, and spectacular and have made me who I am. But, I was no longer getting anything new or positive out of it. I knew drinking was holding me back. Trust me, a much better life awaits you when you leave the party. You will still be capable of having fun without your crutch. You'll still be funny, outgoing, and a good dancer. You'll also save yourself a ton of money, and never being hungover again is reason enough to quit!

We have all been conditioned to drink our whole lives by movies, songs, books, advertising, etc. Some of us grew up with parents who drank. Some of us may have a biological proclivity for booze. There are a million different excuses to drink. Earth is a tough place to live; I get it. Undiluted reality 24/7 is not for the weak of heart and mind. But you will have a much better time by chasing sustainable, positive dopamine instead of the delusory variety you find in a bottle. Whatever motivates you to stop drinking is out there, whether it's physical, financial, or mental. Figure out what that thing is and run with it.

What are you still getting out of drinking? What else besides your money and time is it taking from you? What positive things in your life can you attribute to alcohol? What are you running from or trying to numb by drinking? These are great questions to ask yourself. Not many people are brave enough to step back and take inventory of their lives, but you are better than most! You are not afraid to look into the eyes of the beast and say, "Hey! Fuck you, man! I don't need you anymore!"

~ HAVE A PLAN

When you begin your journey, have a plan. You cannot break a habit without replacing it with another. Boredom is the quickest way back to the bottle. The amount of time you gain back (especially if you drink like I did) is staggering. You will have a difficult time if you're unprepared to fill those gaps with something else. Exercise, reading, taking up new or old hobbies, enrolling in a class for something you've always wanted to pursue; the options are limitless. Get creative with how you want to spend all the extra time you're getting back from the thieving hands of alcohol. They say it takes 21 days for a new habit to stick. I'd respectfully disagree and give it 90. If something isn't holding your interest, pick something else. There are no rules to this game except:

DON'T GET BORED!

Sad fact: I was badly hungover at least two days out of the week. On some of those days, I was completely bedridden from a drug comedown. That means I've spent nearly six years' worth of days being hungover when you add that up after two decades.

~ HEALTH FIRST

If you are science-minded, start by diving into all the data on how alcohol affects the body. It's one of the most corrosive substances you can ingest. It's literally poison. Do you know what the most dangerous and damaging drug is according to global statistics? The one more destructive than heroin, crack, meth, cocaine, tobacco? The number one thing you can use to wreak the most havoc in all aspects of your life? You guessed it; alcohol! If all the diseases, maladies, and toll on your physical appearance, mental stability, and finances aren't enough to dissuade you, how about the quality of your sleep? If you aren't sleeping well, you aren't doing anything well. The initial punch of alcohol can make you drowsy and fall asleep; however, you aren't getting the restorative REM sleep your brain and body needs to recover from the day. Just one glass of wine at night is enough to disrupt your slumber. As a result, you may be irritable, forgetful, or lethargic and feel like you're in an overall slump. If you are prone to depression, sleep deprivation will exacerbate your symptoms.

Have you ever been told you snore like a flu-ridden Sasquatch when you drink? I have. I annoyed everyone within a mile radius of me when I snored. Having your significant other leave you to rest in the serenity of the couch in another room isn't a good feeling. Getting whacked in the head by bandmates in the tour van to wake you up sucks. Nobody wants to hear your alcohol-induced sleep apnea. I went on a few tours with a band whose singer snored just as bad, if not worse, than me. When we got to a hotel, the other guys would banish us into a different room they nicknamed the "snore tank." If I had just one drink in the evening, I would wake up several times during the night. That's because even a tiny amount of alcohol will trigger sleep apnea. If you're unfamiliar with that, it's when you stop breathing in your sleep, and your brain wakes you up to remind your dumb ass to breathe. Your body is trying to kill you for having that nightcap.

When I stopped drinking, my snoring was significantly reduced, and the quality of my sleep improved dramatically. Getting out of bed in the morning was no longer a struggle. The feeling of waking up thoroughly restored, well-rested, and running at 100% is better than any drunk or high you can buy. Imagine if that Bloody Mary, Michelada, or bump of coke the morning after a long night of "having fun" made you feel as good as getting a full eight hours of quality sleep. How much would you pay for such a drug? How much would you spend to not feel the way you do after a night of partying? I bet you'd pay much more than what you spent to "have a good time." I know I would've.

The good news is that feeling is free! Getting a good night's sleep is life-changing. You are making things so much harder for yourself running on fumes. The untapped potential you waste because you are tired is immeasurable. It keeps you stuck in your rut. Are you at a job you don't like, but it gets you by? Maybe you don't even drink that much on the weekends, but just enough to make you slightly hungover or drag your feet in the morning. Chances are you are not looking to sharpen your skills or learn new ones for a better career. It makes you complacent with mediocrity. Work, drink, repeat. The opportunity cost you pay is more devastating to your life than anything else.

To illustrate my point, let's say you and a friend set out to walk three miles daily for a year. You're not getting adequate rest some nights because of the glass of wine you had to "relax," and on the weekends, you're sluggish because you're mildly hungover. You still put in the effort and crank out two miles daily, only one shy of the goal. At the end of the year, your friend who got a good night's sleep, including weekends, has walked 365 miles further than you. That's a massive amount of wasted potential. If you're giving up two hours of productivity every day because you aren't feeling the best you could be, you've thrown out thirty days at the end of a year. What would you do with an extra month of life?

If you are tired, you are less likely to exercise and eat properly. When was the last time you worked out and had a healthy breakfast after a night of drinking? *Never*, you say? I'm shocked! Does ordering delivery and spending the day on the couch sound more realistic? The days I threw away because I was tired and hungover are too many to count. It's not worth it. Good sleep is the catalyst for a positive swing in momentum. If you wake up feeling like a champion, you will act like a champion. If you behave like a champion, you will become a fucking champion! So, get some quality sleep, you magnificent champion!

Better sleep, Better life!

~ REINVENT YOURSELF

Are you afraid to stop drinking because it's part of your identity? And if so, which identity are you concerned about? Nobody shares the one you have in your head about yourself. No two people have the same opinion of who you are as a person, not even your parents. Or, maybe you're scared you won't have fun anymore. Your other buddies seem to be handling their drinking okay, so why can't I? These are some of the thoughts that kept me chained to my vices. First off, nobody gives a fuck about your self-imposed "identity." That's something I learned pretty quick. I had imagined fantasies about how people would react to the news of me quitting drinking, and they resembled nothing like the responses I got. At first, I didn't tell anybody what I was up to. As I mentioned previously, my journey to stop drinking wasn't premeditated. A sidewalk whacked it into my face. I didn't think I'd make it past two weeks without a beer. I didn't want to tell anyone in case it didn't work out. I was afraid of looking like a failure. I came out of the closet, so to speak, around the three-week mark when I was absolutely sure I wasn't returning to Liquorville.

The responses I received were all positive. "Damn that's crazy" were the least enthusiastic reactions. But beyond that, it was all good vibes. I received a lot of "Yeah, I've been trying to cut back myself" reactions. That response is the best because it's a subconscious compliment. It's the same when you tell someone you started exercising, eating better, or reading more. You will usually hear, "Yeah, I've been trying to do that too." That's because the person you're speaking with also wants to be doing positive, healthy things.

The reactions were also, in a way, underwhelming. It's not the breaking news you think it's going to be. Everybody is in their own head and doing their own thing. The universe is indifferent to us all. I wasn't seen without a drink in my hand for twenty years. I thought people would react like I had lost a limb or grown another. But alas, that was not the case. It was acknowledged, and everyone moved on with their lives. Your true friends will be the ones who are continually inspiring and encouraging. And that's a fantastic feeling!

As far as fun goes, I won't lie to you; that takes adjustment. I couldn't do anything without drinking. If I went somewhere I knew didn't serve alcohol, I'd bring my own and drink before I went, or I would find something else to do. I couldn't make a phone call to a friend without having a beer. Sometimes, I'd even prioritize drinking over sex. If you drink as much as I did, your baseline to feel like a normal person requires a drink or four. I used to think that alcohol allowed me to be a more authentic version of myself, but that was not the case at all. It turned me into one of those amusement park, grossly out-of-proportion cartoon caricatures of someone vaguely resembling me. If I went somewhere, and they didn't serve booze (god forbid!) and I didn't properly prepare for such a scenario, I would freak the fuck out. My patience would be gone within minutes. I would get extremely uncomfortable and turn into an irritable, whiney asshole. It was a glaring sign that I was not in control anymore.

The first couple of nondrinking hangouts with friends were strange. I didn't know how to be me. I definitely felt the emptiness of the gaps that drinking would usually fill. Keeping things short helps as you adjust to your new, authentic self. Meeting for an hour or two is a great way to dip your toe into this new lagoon. Activities are another way to keep things interesting, so you're not so self-conscious: playing pool or any type of game or sport, hiking, shows, movies. Whatever keeps you in motion will make your hang time with friends feel more natural. Having non-alcoholic beers or "mocktails" is another excellent way to take the edge off. The alcohol-free beverage options nowadays are incredible. They taste great and provide a placebo-like effect. And if you feel uncomfortable, being honest and letting people know how you're feeling is always encouraged.

It took a few months for me to feel normal around friends. If you still hang out with people who are drinking, you'll notice how rapidly their composure deteriorates. When you realize how ridiculous people behave while drunk, you will not want to be around them. The idea of having drinks to debase yourself to their level is a thought you will not entertain. It's reinforcement for sticking to your new lifestyle because it's a reminder of how you used to act. You were not the life of the party or master of flirtation you thought you were.

~ DON'T COMPARE

Do not compare yourself to anybody else. If you have buddies who seem to be in control of their drinking and have the perfect balance, it doesn't mean that you can. Everybody is wired differently. What's good for them may kill you. For example, I've smoked and snorted crystal methamphetamine several times in my life. It wasn't my first choice of narcotic, but if cocaine wasn't around, it would suffice. I never particularly liked it, but I had a couple of friends who tried it once and never returned from the claws of that beast. I've seen firsthand how meth destroys lives. Why didn't it ruin me too? Of course, other people could stop drinking after a few rounds, and I could not. It's all luck of the biological draw. My point is—it doesn't matter how anybody does anything differently than you. It has no bearing on your compulsions or control. How they metabolize drugs and drink, how diet and exercise affect their bodies, or how fast they pick up a skill or learn something new has nothing to do with how you will do it. You cannot go by appearances, either. The in-control, smiling facade you see could be hiding a warehouse full of demons. You never know what's going through someone's head, so don't judge a burrito by its tortilla. Fuck what everyone else is doing. Life is not a competition. Do what feels right for you.

If you fill your day pursuing goals, reading, exercising, and live an overall healthy lifestyle, your brain will produce dopamine, which is the thing you are chasing with drinking and drugs. When you feel good about yourself, everything else falls into place. You will feel comfortable being social because you will be more confident in your skin. When you radiate confidence, you become magnetic. People will gravitate towards you. It's not an overnight change, but taking even the most minor step toward a new goal, routine, or diet is a step in the right direction. Having fun and being your authentic self is the byproduct of better choices.

"You're under no obligation to be the same person you were five minutes ago."
-Alan Watts

~ FIND YOURSELF

Life is short and is void of a quantifiable, universally agreed on purpose. Reality is hard to stomach without aid. Painful, intrusive thoughts steal your peace and make you miserable. Having a temporary reprieve from oneself feels necessary to implement. Dulling the pain of a long day or week with a few cold ones seems mandatory. *Why shouldn't I drink? We all die; nothing ultimately matters, and I just want to have fun!* This sentiment is often used as justification for self-destructive behavior. I know this because it was the First Amendment in my mission statement. Although the fact that our time here is short, and the reason for our miniscule contribution to the cosmos may never be known, it is not an excuse to be your worst self.

Many recovery and rehabilitation programs can have a religious, theistic stink on them. My aim isn't to sell you my philosophical beliefs, but I do think it's essential that I share mine to give you a complete understanding of my thought process. My personal philosophies amalgamate many different concepts—Stoicism, Taoism, Buddhism, Humanism, Agnosticism, Absurdism, Determinism, and even a pinch of Existential Nihilism, to name a few. I have a sense of spirituality and a feeling of universal connectedness without having a definable "god." (The word "spirit" comes from the Latin *spiritus*, meaning "breath"—i.e., "life.") These elements create the magnetic pull to keep my moral compass pointing north. They gave me courage, comfort, and strength when I began to make monumental changes in my life and kept me on course for continual self-improvement.

God is an abstract concept that lives solely in your head. Even if you shared the same faith with someone, you would not share an identical god—much like no one will hear a song the exact same way you do, or be moved by a piece of art in the same way. It's a personal interpretation constructed by our biology and every single thing that has ever happened to us. I think God is the name you give to your ideal, most perfect self. The person you ultimately want to act, look, feel, and be like is living in your brain and gives you clues on how to get closer to them. When you wake up hungover and look into the mirror, that disappointment, shame, or regret you may feel comes from this god-self. You cannot lie, cheat, or escape its scrutiny because it's you. It knows all, sees all, and wants the very best for you. It also means that all the discipline, strength, and willpower you'll ever need is already a facet of your personality that you have yet to uncover. You are not helpless. You just need to be radically honest with yourself and get angry with your own bullshit. That is the way to your internal divinity.

Praying is another way of saying manifesting, internalizing, visualizing, or meditating. It works no matter what you want to call it. Remember: you are trying to reach your perfect self when you do this. Verbalizing or writing your thoughts down helps to sort them out and gives you a clearer picture of the dialogue inside your head. But you cannot wish or pray for a better life; you must work for it. If you want to get in better shape, I will slap the pie out of your hand and take you to the gym. I will not tell you you're helpless and damaged and that if you pray hard enough, the lord will give you six-pack abs. If you'd like to get better at an instrument, skill, or sport, just reading about it only helps so much. You have to practice what you've learned. Belief in yourself and what you are capable of is a critical component of your success. What you fucked up yesterday can only be improved by what you do today. The wake of a ship does not influence the direction it's going.

All the advice and therapy you receive won't mean anything if you don't act upon it. Seeking out a support group, therapist, rabbi, personal trainer, or voodoo priestess can help, but only if you implement what you've learned into your daily life. No one walks out of an IKEA with an entertainment center. You walk out with a box full of all the components and directions to assemble an entertainment center. It's up to you to put it together. You have to be willing, committed, and disciplined to put in the work. I found all my strength and comfort in books and YouTube videos, but there would have been no change if I hadn't put what I had learned into action. If your goal is not to drink anymore, all you have to do is not put anything alcoholic in your mouth. It's that simple. The hard part is navigating the thoughts around not drinking. Beyond medication or being physically restrained, your willpower is the only way to do that. You are the only one who can save you.

Creating and believing in your specific purpose is essential to your well-being and survival. It is not something that anyone or anything assigns to you. It is up to you to manifest and make it your driving force. You can have multiple purposes during your life and create new ones as you see fit. If something stops working for you, end it and move on. Being rigid about a belief or a lifestyle is limiting and foolish if it no longer makes sense or doesn't give you peace. The last few years I drank, I didn't believe I had a purpose and was just going through the motions as a sentient automaton. I had strayed so far from my ideal self (god) that I lost sight of who I was supposed to be. I was ingesting poison because I was afraid to have an honest, introspective analysis of who I was.

Working on myself was my first priority. I focused on the roots of my thoughts and actions. *Why* do I think the things I think, and do the things I do? If I got hung up on a particular issue, I knew it was because I wasn't asking the right questions or looking at it from the proper angle. I wasn't happy with myself or the world I had created. I needed to put better ideas in my head and learn to frame situations and even life differently—books on basic psychology, and philosophy without dogma helped tremendously. Positive change comes from the inside out. Getting your head straight is the first thing you must do. If you're open and receptive to alternate mind-expanded methods such as meditation, psilocybin, or hypnosis, I highly recommend pursuing those avenues. Even Bill Wilson, co-founder of AA, found LSD to be a vital part of his journey toward enlightenment. (It's recommended that any use of psychoactive substances be done in a controlled environment with an experienced guide.) Whatever it takes to sort your head out is critical. You cannot control what happens to you, only how you react to what happens to you. Your path to higher consciousness starts with education. Conceptualize, visualize, and intellectualize your thoughts and behaviors. Put yourself under a microscope and make self-improvement your first purpose.

Get closer to your divine self!

~ BELIEVE IN YOURSELF

Please note: *I'm not bashing any program, rehab, or recovery methods. Much like diets, exercise regimens, gods/ religions, or flavors of ice cream, there isn't one thing on this planet that everyone will agree on. Although AA didn't resonate with me, it has been an indispensable resource for millions of people over the decades, and I would not dissuade anyone from seeking their help.*

I don't believe I'm a helpless victim. I was complicit in all my habits and crimes. I don't accept that I'm powerless regarding my resolve and strength of character. These are some of the issues I have with the twelve-step program. I do agree with admitting you have a problem and taking personal inventory. That's where this journey needs to begin. It's also necessary to own and admit to your mistakes. But at the end of the day, you and you alone have to overcome your problem(s). You must learn more about your mind and how addiction works, to break the chain of destructive habits.

If you believe you are damaged and powerless, you will act damaged and powerless. If someone (or yourself) calls you a piece of shit every day, you might internalize that and start to believe it. Telling someone they're inherently flawed and incapable of doing something can have profoundly negative effects. I think it gives people an excuse not to try as hard as they would otherwise. The clinical term for this cognitive behavior is "illusory truth syndrome." Determination, will, and unrelenting spirit against adversity win the day. How many doctors have been wrong when telling someone they'll never walk again because the patient would not accept the diagnosis? Belief in yourself can produce miracles.

Alcohol greatly diminishes the quality of life for millions of people who would not consider themselves "alcoholic" or "problematic drinkers". I think this is why many people don't seek help–they don't want to be put into that box. This is my issue with the semantics. There is ample data on the use of specific language when it comes to SUDs (substance use disorders). Some notable information comes from the National Institute of Drug Abuse (NIDA), the American Society of Addiction Medicine (ASAM), and The National Council for Mental Wellbeing—to name a few. I took it a step further and added a couple more descriptors I don't like associating myself with.

I don't identify as being "sober," nor do I practice "sobriety." I'm not "in recovery," "diseased," an "addict" or "alcoholic." Drinking was making my life chaotic and intolerable, so I stopped drinking. That's the end of the story. No suggestive labels are needed. I had problems when I drank, but I no longer think about alcohol, much less struggle with compulsions to drink. I don't need a specific name or a giant scarlet A painted on my forehead to remind me of the ghosts of my past. If I found myself lost in the woods, I wouldn't hesitate to admit I was lost and would seek help in any way, shape, or form. But after I made it out safely, I would not anchor myself to the identity of someone who gets lost in the woods, nor do I need to be terminally "recovering" from it. I will simply avoid the fucking woods! I don't see any benefit in stamping yourself with stigma-riddled adjectives that carry negative connotations; for example, if I said I was an ex-con (which, technically I am) or a member of the Manson family, you'd immediately have some sort of judgment about my moral failings. Deliberate language is essential for you to speak and for people to hear. The difference between me saying, "I don't drink anymore," or "I'm not a drinker," versus "I'm a recovering alcoholic" is massive. The "I don't drink" statements declare independence, transcendence, and empowerment, whereas the latter are compunctions and imply that I'm permanently flawed. Not only are there no particular labels for people who quit smoking or lost a lot of weight, but their achievements are met with admiration. The same nonjudgmental enthusiasm isn't applied to someone deemed an "addict" or "alcoholic." I don't have an issue discussing my past, but there's no reason to be chained to it. Besides, if I had to choose a moniker, it would be something cooler, like "alcohol transcender" or "party veteran."

Say it:
I am not a drinker!
I don't drink anymore!

~ VISUALIZE YOUR GOALS

Visualization and reverse engineering are potent tools to help you on your way. Think of where you want to be and who you want to be. What changes do you need to make now to get to that destination? What traits, habits, and impulses can you tweak to become the person you'd be proud of? When you learn to be more mindful of what triggers you and the thought patterns you have on autopilot, you can start to change them as they arise.

Picture a soundboard with all the different nobs and faders that adjust the highs, lows, and mids. If you are unfamiliar with what that looks like, imagine the different adjustments you can make when editing a photo (shadows, contrast, sharpness, filters) or an attribute bar in a video game (strength, stamina, speed). On a soundboard, these controls aim to get the best possible balance of frequencies to make the music you hear sound the most optimal. Now consider the same kind of apparatus can be used to manipulate your emotions, impulses, and personality traits. What adjustments can you make to get the perfect sound, or in this case, self?

When I'm present and aware of my automatic emotional impulses that need adjusting, I picture twisting a dial on an equalizer that controls the specific emotion or action I'd like to change. Someone cuts you off in traffic, and you want to rip their leg off and beat them with it? Maybe turn down your anger a pinch. Are you afraid to ask for a raise or strike up a conversation with a stranger? Turn that confidence up a little. Are you not exercising, keeping your home clean, or attending to your hygiene like you should? Slide those dignity and self-respect faders up. To adjust my emotional response to the appropriate degree for any situation, I visualize turning a dial tethered to the emotion I want to refine. When I was drinking, my eternal EQ was making my personal soundtrack unlistenable, not only to me but to everyone else. My emotions were completely out of whack. When I figured out the only way to make this thing sound good was to take the alcohol out of the mix, it was a no-brainer. It became something I had to do.

You are the engineer recording the album of your life. There will be fast, slow, sad, happy, and everything in-between types of songs, but they will all have one thing in common: how they are mixed and mastered. As an engineer, you will get better at this on a daily basis if you pay attention and learn from your mistakes. Is your record going gold, platinum, or diamond? It's up to you. Just remember, hit records aren't recorded overnight. You will have to navigate through several obstacles, challenges, and variables. Your album, (your life) is your story. Make the very best effort you can. It's the only one you're ever going to create.

You are the creator of your destiny!

~ NEVER GIVE UP

Be tenacious and relentless toward your goal. If an obstacle arises, get creative about how to overcome it. I played a show in a small town in the Netherlands once, and unbeknownst to us, the whole village stopped selling alcohol at an early hour. We had gone through all the beer and liquor we had, and there was seemingly no way to get more. We stayed at a strange property in the middle of nowhere with cabins and campsites strewn about the woods. The night was relatively young, and we were still up and wanted to party. Not accepting this predicament, my bandmate and I concocted a plan to go cabin-to-cabin like it was Halloween and offered Euros to anybody willing to part with their alcohol. Not only did we gather all kinds of different beverages, but we also met some really cool and bizarre people. On our last stop, we even scored some LSD!

The moral here is that if you are locked in on a goal and unwilling to accept your current circumstance, get creative and stop at nothing. I can't tell you how many times I pulled off seemingly impossible feats just to get alcohol, drugs, or cigarettes. I'd climb mountains and part seas if that's what it took. The energy, creativity, and persistence were already inside me; I just had to redirect it toward something positive. Think about your life and the times you stopped at nothing to get what you wanted, no matter how trivial. We are all capable of creating astounding outcomes if we put our whole heart and mind into it. Whatever change you want is within your grasp if you want it bad enough.

Don't give up!

~ LIVE WITH GRATITUDE

Gratitude and passion for life, friends, and family will guide you toward your better self. Take a moment out of your day to reflect on your body and health. You should be immensely grateful if you're able to function without assistance. If you have food, shelter, and running water, you are doing better than a couple of billion people worldwide who would desperately want your privileges. We all have the capacity to be a positive influence in someone's life, no matter how large or small. It's our duty to do it. If your drinking is fucking up anything at all, you need to take a hard look at what you love and cherish and determine what's worth losing for alcohol.

I get knots in my stomach when I remember times I exhibited repugnant, inexcusable behavior toward anyone I loved (or anyone at all) because I was buzzed, drunk, or hungover. I was rarely grateful for anyone and anything when I drank. Alcohol never allowed me to have a deep understanding of how important the people in my life are or my overwhelming good fortune. I placed drinking in front of my health and the contribution I made toward my friends and family. If I had taken a second to realize just how much love and gratitude I had for the people around me, I might have stopped drinking much sooner.

I was intensely thankful for all the relationships that remained after I quit alcohol. Everything that I didn't burn to the ground became precious to me. Becoming the best version of myself was my only option after seeing the world through the lens of gratitude. To have the audacity to jeopardize my health, and the bonds with the people I love, over a drink is inconceivable to me now.

Don't mistake your drunken, exaggerated emotions for passion. I used to think that drinking made me feel music more intensely, or love for my friends or significant other with greater depth, but it didn't. All it did was give me a temporary insincere enthusiasm. It distorts the actual reality of whatever you're engaged with. It diminishes all the delicate nuances that make a person or work of art whole and complete. You develop a more profound appreciation for whatever you're beholding when you understand someone or something with granular detail.

I was afraid I'd lose the fire inside me after I stopped drinking. Like I'd just shrivel up and become a lifeless husk of the person I used to be, submitting to the status quo as an indentured servant until life's last act of kindness (death) carried my soul across the River Styx. But nothing could be farther from the truth. The zest and fervor I had for my existence became more authentic and vivid with every day further apart from alcohol. Passion and gratitude are amplified when you allow yourself to be vulnerable and open to love something for what or who it truly is.

So hug your friends and fucking mean it! Say I love you and fucking mean it! Make love with ravenous hunger! Throw yourself wholeheartedly into whatever makes every atom in your body vibrate with genuine excitement! Do it with passion and gratitude. Don't dilute the beauty of your existence and become a watered-down, half-assed version of the person you're supposed to be.

Live with Passion and Gratitude!

~ Flow with the ever-changing tides of life.

Lastly, I want you to have courage and believe in yourself. Life is complicated and confusing, no matter who you are. Sorting out your thoughts and emotions is the most crucial thing you can do to have an easier time here on earth. Your perspectives, values, and limits are all in your head. Nobody's opinion of you will make you better or worse. Crave validation from your inner, ideal self before anyone else. Looking back, I can clearly see how insecure and afraid I was of simply being me. All the outrageous, sometimes disgusting, things I did was merely an act. I drank because I didn't have the confidence to face the real me, and I was afraid to be disliked. I put on a mask and created an arrogant character to protect myself. At first, drinking was a way to bond with friends and ramp up the fun, but then it turned into sweeping my problems under the rug. I never took the time to nurture and cultivate my authentic self.

I felt like this was all I was and could ever be. I lost all hope and purpose. The last year I drank, I constantly felt this eerie feeling of impending doom, like all the shadows, wherever I was, were closing in and suffocating me. Whenever I closed my eyes at night, my head spun with the darkest thoughts, making it difficult to sleep. Not only did I feel like a failure, I felt like everybody was expecting me to fail. Every morning, getting out of bed and functioning became increasingly difficult. There was no light at the end of the tunnel. How many rock bottoms can I hit before I finally break?

It wasn't until I got so angry with myself and couldn't bear the sight of my own reflection that I changed. "You can do this! You are better than this!" became mantras. I gathered all the courage and confidence I could muster up, and put myself under a microscope to see all the bullshit I tried to drown for twenty years. I needed to dissect every little problem one by one in order to move forward. I realized no one was ever coming to save me—it was up to me to do all the work.

When I finally stopped drinking, I realized I had been keeping myself trapped in a little dark, miserable room inside my head the whole time. When I got the courage to walk out, it dawned on me that I could've left whenever I wanted. Inside our minds, we all have a vast landscape full of rooms we can access at all times. Some are light, and some are dark; some are filled with memories we have forgotten or tried to forget. The pathways are adorned with pictures and mementos of the past that we have collected over the years. The thing to remember is that you are free to move about as you see fit. There are no locks on any of the doors. Every mood, emotion, and memory has value, but each is part of the whole; none are permanent states. If you look closely enough, even the most beautiful mosaic will have a few individually ugly tiles within it, but they are necessary to the entire picture.

Your courage and confidence aren't at the bottom of a bottle; they never were. When the lights are out, all the ghosts and monsters in your room don't disappear when you pull the covers over your head; you must face them to be free of their presence. Change isn't easy, but your life may depend on it. I know mine did. All the confidence and courage you'll ever need is somewhere within you–it's just a matter of digging as deep as you can and not stopping until you find it. Be present, move with purpose and urgency, and remember that you are no good to anyone else until you are good to yourself first.

It's last call, stupid… Let's close out, cut our losses, and get the fuck out of here. A much better life is just one step in a new direction.

LAST CALL, STUPID

AN EXIT SRATEGY FROM TOXIC DRINKING CULTURE

JOSHUA DEEN

I am sincerely grateful to all those who have been my constant source of encouragement over the past five years. This writing journey has been a cathartic one. It allowed me to revisit some hilariously embarrassing situations and many long-forgotten memories that brought me so much joy. It also forced me to confront and relive some heart-wrenching and deeply disturbing moments from my past which I'm so grateful to have healed and transcended from. I wanted to be uncomfortably honest, hoping this could help someone get out of their trap, so I held nothing back on these pages. If anyone is struggling with their addictions or mental health to the point of not wanting to go on, please seek professional help. These seemingly insurmountable obstacles can be traversed with the proper perspectives. There is always someone out there that wants to listen to you—never give up hope!

Life isn't over when you give up drinking; life begins.

Acknowledgments

I'd like to thank **Trey Derbes** for formatting and designing a book beyond anything I could have imagined. Your visual design and photography expertise made this a stunning work of art. A huge thanks to **Mikaela Hudson** for proofreading and giving me guidance that brought this book to the highest standard possible. Thanks to the brilliantly talented, **Madeline Bridenbaugh** for your edits, making this the absolute best it could be. Working with my friends was truly a fantastic experience. Having intimate knowledge with my collaborators made this a profoundly fulfilling voyage. Thank you for your encouragement, support, and friendship. Love you!

Thank you to my editor, **Andie Woodard.** Your suggestions and insight gave me the polish to make this thing shine. It was a pleasure working with you.

NOTABLE RESOURCES

Here is a list of Authors, Podcasters, and YouTubers who were vital to my success:

Sam Harris
Alan Watts
Dale Carnegie
Gary John Bishop
Robert Greene
James Clear
Mel Robbins
Kevin O'Hara
Terence McKenna
Dax Shepard
Carl Jung
Lao Tzu
Ryan Holiday
Robert Pantano
Viktor Frankl
Jordan Peterson
Stephen Covey
Theo Von

Amy Morin
Thibaut Meurisse
Andrew Huberman
David Goggins
Jim Rohn
David Robson
Tony Robbins
James Doty
Daniel Walter
Jim Kwik
Friedrich Nietzsche
David Robson
Bertrand Russell
Marcus Aurelius
Nick Trenton
Maxwell Maltz
Mark Manson
Steve O

Made in the USA
Las Vegas, NV
26 September 2024

95844840R00105